Library Use

A Handbook for Psychology

Jeffrey G. Reed
and
Pam M. Baxter

 American Psychological Association
Washington, DC 20036

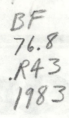

Copies may be ordered from:
Order Department
American Psychological Association
1200 Seventeenth Street, N.W.
Washington, DC 20036

Library of Congress Cataloging in Publication Data
Main entry under author:

Reed, Jeffrey G., 1948–
    Library use.

    Bibliography: p. 124
    Includes index.
    1. Psychological literature.   2. Psychology—Library
resources.   3. Psychological research.   I. Baxter,
Pam M., 1955–   .   II. Title.   [DNLM: 1. Psychology—
Handbooks.   2. Research—Methods—Handbooks.   3. Libraries
—Handbooks.   4. Reference books—Bibliography.   BF 76.5
R324L]
BF76.8.R43 1983   025.5′6′02415   83–12246
ISBN 0–912704–76–4

Text design by Elizabeth Elliott, Concepts Unlimited,
    Washington, DC
Cover Design by Marti Burton, Burton Rudd and Associates,
    Oakton, Virginia
Composition by York Custom Graphics, York, Pennsylvania
Printing by Banta Company/George Banta Company, Inc.,
    Menasha, Wisconsin

Table of Contents

continued

Acknowledgments

Many people—psychologists, librarians, students, and others—assisted with this project. Margaret Matlin was a continuing source of advice and encouragement from the development of the initial prospectus through the reading of numerous chapter drafts. Psychologists Monica Brien, Lawrence Casler, and Kathleen Ferguson provided many helpful comments on chapter drafts. Monica and Kathy suggested Appendix B. Arlene Dempsey, Kathleen McGowan, and David Parish offered feedback from a librarian's perspective whereas Mary Joan Parise and Paddy Berson provided suggestions from a student's point of view. We also received advice on this project from Karen Duffy, Jerry Meyer, Paul Olczak, Lanna Ruddy, and Gregory Trautt. Throughout the entire project, Sylvia Reed has been especially supportive, offering useful advice at many points. Harriet Sleggs typed the prospectus and drafts of several early chapters, and Nancy Smith did a splendid job of typing the final manuscript. Contacts with Virginia O'Leary, Brenda Bryant, and others at APA have been both productive and pleasant, and we are delighted with the technical assistance provided by Ellen Dykes, Separate Publications editor.

Because we made heavy use of the libraries at the State University of New York College at Geneseo, the University of Rochester, and the Rochester Institute of Technology, we thank the staff members of all three libraries.

There are also people from our dark, distant pasts who, although they did not contribute directly to this project, enabled us to execute it—Roberta Armstrong, Jerry Kidd, Andy Armitage, Bob Haro, Paul Wasserman, Donald P. Hoyt, Frank Saal, Richard Halsey, Ann Prentice, staff of the Bucknell University Library, staff at Towson State University, and many others. To all of these people, and to the many who were not aware that they were helping us, we owe a debt of gratitude for they helped make this book a reality.

Jeffrey G. Reed
Pam M. Baxter

Publication Credits

We would like to thank the following publishers for permission to reprint copyrighted materials as noted:

American Psychological Association for our Figures 4–A and 4–B from the *Thesaurus of Psychological Index Terms*, 3rd edition, 1982, pp. 77, 94, 212, 216; our Figure 4–C from *Psychological Abstracts*, Volume 65, June 1981, pp. xvi, xxxix, 1225; our Figure 4–D from *Psychological Abstracts*, Volume 64, 1980, p. 511, and *Psychological Abstracts Semi-Annual Index*, Volume 62 (No. 6, part 2), December 1980, pp. 12, 596; our Figure 4–E from *Psychological Abstracts*, Volume 41, 1967, pp. 865, 1798, 2014, 2318; our Figure 4–F from *Cumulated Author Index to Psychological Abstracts, 1969–1971*, p. 545; our Figure 4–G from *Psychological Abstracts*, Volume 62, 1979, p. 1323; our Figure 4–H from *Psychological Abstracts*, Volume 54, 1975, p. 162; our Figure 4–I from *Psychological Abstracts*, Volume 53, 1975, p. 943, and Volume 62, 1979, p. 1143; our Figure 4–J from *Psychological Abstracts*, Volume 64, 1980, p. 1002; our Figure 8–B from *Psychological Abstracts*, Volume 66, 1981, p. 307, and Semi-Annual Subject Index, July–December, 1981, p. 987 and from the PsycINFO database; and our Table 4–A from *Psychological Abstracts Information Services: Users Reference Manual*, 1981, p. 1–1. Reprinted by permission.

BioSciences Information Service for our Figure 5–L from *Biological Abstracts Semiannual Cumulative Index*, Volume 70, July–December 1980, pp. 1493, 1766; and for our Figure 5–M from *Biological Abstracts*, December 15, 1980, 70(12), p. 8332. Copyright © 1980, 1981 by Biological Abstracts®. Reprinted by permission.

DIALOG® Information Services, Inc., for the format of our Figure 8–B from DIALOG Databases. Reprinted by permission.

Infordata International, Inc., for our Figure 7–D from the *Index to U.S. Government Periodicals*, 1981, p. 30. Reprinted by permission of Infordata International, Inc., Chicago, IL.

Institute for Scientific Information for our Figures 6–A and 6–B from *Social Sciences Citation Index® 1980 Annual*, 1981, Volume 1, p. 6422, and Volume 3, p. 2850. Copyright 1981 by the Institute for Scientific Information. Reprinted by permission.

Macmillan Publishing Company for our Figures 5–D and 5–E from the *Current Index to Journals in Education: Semiannual Cumulation*, January–June 1977, pp. 534, 737. Copyright © 1977 by Macmillan Publishing Company. Reprinted by permission.

Oryx Press for our Figure 5–A from the *Thesaurus of ERIC Descriptors*, 9th ed., 1982, pp. 87, 328; our Figure 5–B from the *Resources in Education Annual Cumulation: Index 1980*, 1981, p. 225; our Figure 5–C from *Resources in Education*, Volume 15, December 1980, p. 36; and our Figures 5–D and 5–E from *Current Index to Journals in Education: Semiannual Cumulation*, January–June 1977, pp. 534, 737. Reprinted by permission of The Oryx Press, 2214 North Central at Encanto, Phoenix, AZ 85004.

Sociological Abstracts, Inc., for our Figure 5—H from the *Cumulative Subject Index of Sociological Abstracts*, Volume 24, 1976, pp. 1318, 1319, 1385; and for our Figure 5—I from *Sociological Abstracts*, April 1976, *24*(1), p. 193. Copyright 1976 by Sociological Abstracts, Inc. Reprinted by permission.

University Microfilms International for Figure 11—C from *Dissertation Abstracts International*, Volume 34, 1974, pp. 4489—4490. Reprinted by permission.

University of Nebraska Press for our Figure 9—A from the *Eighth Mental Measurements Yearbook*, Volume 1, 1978, p. 867. Copyright © 1978 by Gryphon Press, Highland Park, NJ. Reprinted by permission of the University of Nebraska Press.

H. W. Wilson Company for our Figure 5—F from *Education Index*, December 1981, *53*(4), p. 119; and our Figure 5—G from *Business Periodicals Index: 1980—1981 Annual Cumulation*, Volume 23, p. 1228. Education Index Copyright © 1981 by The H. W. Wilson Company. Business Periodicals Index Copyright © 1980, 1981, 1982 by The H. W. Wilson Company. Materials reproduced by permission of the publisher.

Additionally, we have included numerous illustrations from publications in the public domain prepared by the **Educational Resources Information Center, U.S. National Library of Medicine, U.S. Government Printing Office, and U.S. Library of Congress.**

1 Introduction: Getting Started

Reasons for Writing This Book

A library is a storehouse for information recorded over the years. Observations, reflections, empirical data, theories, and so forth are continually reported in books, journals, and other forms by researchers in many fields. Some of this knowledge you will examine in your formal education. A variety of important problems and issues will be dealt with in a textbook chapter or two or during several meeting sessions of a course; some prominent topics may involve a whole course. But there is much information to which you will never be exposed in a classroom; and you will find some issues that you must pursue on your own. Your immediate need for information may stem from a research paper that you have to write for which you must use the library.

We have found that most students have little formal training in the use of the library. Typically, a student's experience is limited to a superficial exposure to the card catalog, a periodical index, and the reserve desk to complete assigned class-readings. Consequently, when confronted with a topic necessitating more extensive use of the library, many students fail to locate the information needed.

Although faculty members generally recognize students' need to obtain psychological literature, many are hesitant to assume the task of teaching library-use skills. Some faculty have never had the benefit of such instruction themselves. Often courses on research methods stress the conduct of empirical research and reporting, allowing little time for instruction in library-use skills. Although some faculty tap the resources of the library's staff to teach such skills, these library sessions usually take only one classroom hour, seldom provide hands-on experience, and offer only a glimpse of the resources available. Thus *Library Use: A Handbook for Psychology* was written to bridge the gap between the need that a student embarking on a psychology research project has for information and the information that is available in the college library.

The Audience

This book is intended as an introduction to library research for college students. It will supplement instruction in library research methods provided in the classroom setting. We anticipate that the typical reader will be enrolled in a college course in experimental psychology or research methods or will be engaged in independent study. The book may be used as a supplement to a textbook on research methods and to the American Psychological Association's *Publication Manual.* It will also be useful to students in other situations involving research projects such as honors papers. Graduate students and faculty may find the information presented about some of the specialized sources to be a useful supplement to their knowledge of bibliographic tools.

Scope and Approach

Library Use concentrates on information sources available in the typical college library (a library of 100,000 to 300,000 volumes serving a college of 2,000 to 5,000 students). It briefly mentions specialized resources important to researchers in particular subfields of psychology that can be found in larger libraries.

We have made few assumptions about a student's library knowledge and library-use skills. The book provides brief background information concerning each type of source discussed and presents a minisearch to illustrate the use of each major source. Numerous figures illustrate the principles and sources discussed.

A Note on Taking Notes

The first step in taking notes is to get a stack of index cards. Some people suggest using computer cards. Others suggest two different sized cards: smaller cards (e.g., 3″ x 5″ or 4″ x 6″) on which to record bibliographic information about sources and larger cards (e.g., 5″ x 8″) on which to take notes about the content of the sources.

Bibliographic information enables you to identify and locate a book, article, or other publication. For books, this information includes the name(s) of the author(s) and editor(s), the title, the place of publication, the publisher, the date of publication, and the call number of the book (for more information about the call number see chapter 3). For articles, full bibliographic information includes the name(s) of the author(s), the article title, the journal name, the year, the volume number, and the page numbers of the article. Become accustomed to recording information as outlined in the American Psychological Association *Publication Manual.* Record the complete bibliographic information for each source on a separate card. Such recording helps ensure accuracy and completeness and saves time later in the research process. Using a separate card for each source allows you to add relevant sources and delete irrelevant sources as needed. This also makes alphabetizing easier when you prepare your reference list for the paper.

In addition, on each index card record the source or reference tool in which you located the information about the article, book, or other publication. This information will be essential if you need to use interlibrary loan (see chapter 11).

When you take notes, use a separate card for each important point in a source and clearly identify exact quotations, taking care to record page numbers. Some people simply make photocopies of sources of interest, which can be useful if the exact wording is needed. If many sources have been identified, however, photocopying can be very expensive. In taking notes, identify the main points and summarize material in your own words. You must read and understand the author's points and not just copy the text. Campbell and Ballou (1978), Sternberg (1977), and Turabian (1976) are a few authors who provide additional suggestions and details on taking notes and writing the paper.

Careful note-taking also helps you avoid inadvertent plagiarism. Plagiarism is a frequent problem in student papers; it is theft. "It means stealing other people's words and ideas and making them appear to be your own" (Pauk, 1974). Therefore, be sure to provide accurate and complete references to the sources of information and ideas contained in your paper. Plagiarism may result in your failing a course or in your expulsion from college. Gibaldi and Achtert (1977) advise that if you have any doubt about whether something constitutes plagiarism, provide a reference.

A Note on Libraries

There is no such thing as a "typical" college library. A library may be large and spacious, small and cramped, comfortable and quiet, or dreary and noisy. Over the years each library has acquired its own collection of materials reflecting interests of the members of that academic community—librarians, faculty, staff, and students. Most importantly, each library has its own organizational quirks and procedures.

Although the actual materials may vary, all libraries contain the same types of materials—reference works, monographs, periodicals, microforms, government publications, audio-visual materials, and so forth. Differences among libraries are largely in the organization of those materials.

The monographic collection consists of those books and series of books that you may borrow from the library. Every library uses some system to arrange and catalog monographs. In most cases this system is a card catalog (see chapter 3).

Serials are publications issued on a regular or an irregular continuing basis. The *Annual Review of Psychology,* published annually as a bound volume, is a monographic serial. The *American Psychologist,* a monthly journal, is another type of serial, known as a periodical. *Psychological Abstracts* (see chapter 4), although a reference tool indexing psychological literature, is a monthly periodical. Periodicals may be classified and shelved with monographs, or they may be arranged alphabetically by periodical title. How does your library handle serials?

All libraries contain staffs of librarians and library assistants and have similar functional departments, although these departments may have different names. The acquisitions department staff orders materials. The cataloging staff determines where materials should be located. The staff of the serials department handles the mountains of daily, weekly, monthly, and annual journals, indexes, abstracts, and so forth. Reference librarians help users find what they need and provide instruction in library use. Interlibrary-loan staff members locate and obtain copies of materials needed by researchers but unavailable in the library. These people strive to provide a library that supports the community in its search for information.

Explore your library! Find out where materials—card catalog, periodicals, and so forth—are located. Where is the reference department? Is there a special information desk? When can you get assistance if you need it? Some libraries offer brief 15- or 20-minute library tours at the beginning of each year. Take advantage of this offer to get acquainted.

A Note About Reference Librarians

In your search for information, you will probably have contact primarily with the reference staff. Often located in a central reference room, reference materials typically include such things as handbooks, bibliographies, dictionaries, encyclopedias, periodical indexes, and abstracts. These materials usually may not be borrowed from the library.

Conscientious reference librarians will be glad to assist you with your project because their job is to help people use the library effectively. Their specialty is information retrieval, not usually a subject such as physiological psychology, cultural anthropology, or organic chemistry. As far as fields of study are concerned, librarians tend to be generalists rather than specialists. This general background provides them with a good overview of many fields, an understanding of how the fields relate to one another, and an ability to search for information in many ways and many places.

When you ask a librarian for assistance, be specific, complete, and timely about what you want. Requesting a particular index does not tell the librarian what you need, only what you think you need. Your list of search terms, the definition of your topic, or some of the relevant sources you have already identified may clarify your actual need. Pressing librarians into service the day before a paper is due does not give them (or you) time to do a thorough job. Start early, allow yourself plenty of time, and avoid the end-of-semester rush. By so doing, you enable a librarian to give your request more time and consideration.

What This Book Does and Does Not Cover

Library Use: A Handbook for Psychology will inform you about sources of information available in college libraries, how these sources are organized, and how to use these sources. Chapters 2, 3, and 4 provide basic information about the principles of library and source organization; subsequent chapters assume that the reader is already familiar with this information. Through several examples chapter 2 discusses defining and limiting the topic, which for many students is the most difficult part of the literature-search process. Chapter 3 concentrates on using the card catalog to establish the presence of monographic materials and finding those materials in the library. Chapter 4 discusses *Psychological Abstracts,* the most important index to psychological journal literature.

Chapter 5 covers important indexes in the related areas of education, management, sociology, and medicine. Whereas chapters 4 and 5 concentrate on subject searches, chapter 6 discusses the author/citation search, which begins with a particular key source. No discussion of libraries would be complete without mention of government publications, especially those of the U.S. federal government. These publications are described in chapter 7. Chapter 8 covers a recent innovation in library service—the computer bibliographic search; chapter 9 covers sources of information on psychological tests and measures. Chapter 10 presents some important but less basic sources of information—sources for current research, book reviews, and biographical sources. Chapter 11 helps the individual who has exhausted the resources of his or her own library by providing alternative sources such as interlibrary loan.

Appendix A lists selected sources not covered elsewhere in this book. The dictionaries, encyclopedias, bibliographies, indexes, and other sources are more specialized and may not be available in your library. Appendix B, designed to be used as a worksheet, provides a step-by-step overview of literature searching.

Library Use will not, however, tell you how to organize or write a paper; for such information, see Campbell and Ballou (1978), Sternberg (1977), or Turabian (1976). For discussions of the form of a psychology paper, proper reference style, and so forth, consult the American Psychological Association's *Publication Manual* (1983). Nor will this book tell you how to perform research other than that involving library materials. For discussions of approaches to empirical research—designing an experiment, constructing a questionnaire, collecting data, analyzing data, and so forth—consult books on research methods or statistics (e.g., Elms, Kantowitz, & Roediger, 1981; Kerlinger, 1973; Wood, 1981).

How To Use This Book

At the beginning of the book, you will find a detailed table of contents, which contains a brief outline for each chapter. This table of contents indicates both the materials in and the organization of each chapter. At the beginning of each chapter, you will find the major sources discussed within that chapter listed in the order of their presentation. References to other materials in each discussion are listed at the end of the chapter. Within each chapter, tables and figures are identified by the chapter number and a sequential letter for each particular table or figure. Some parts in the figures are identified with numbers. Rather than being presented in a key to each figure, these parts, or figure elements, are described and explained in the text, and the corresponding element reference numbers appear in boldface in the text. For your convenience, we have included an index to major sources and important terms at the end of the book.

Throughout *Library Use,* we have emphasized that both knowledge of the bibliographic tools in psychology and search strategy are the keys to the successful literature search. The development of plans for systematic gathering of information is illustrated throughout the book within the context of the sources presented. For this reason, *Library Use* is more than a guide to the literature; it is a tool for learning. After you read a chapter, try to use a source about which you have just read. Practice will reinforce your learning.

References

American Psychological Association. (1983). *Publication manual* (3rd ed.). Washington, DC: Author.

Campbell, W. C., & Ballou, S. W. (1978). *Form and style: Theses, reports, term papers* (5th ed.). Boston: Houghton Mifflin.

Elms, D. G., Kantowitz, B. H., & Roediger, H. L. (1981). *Methods in experimental psychology.* Boston: Houghton Mifflin.

Gibaldi, J., & Achtert, W. S. (1977). *MLA handbook for writers of research papers, theses, and dissertations* (Student ed.). New York: Modern Language Association.

Kerlinger, F. N. (1973). *Foundations of behavioral research* (2nd ed.). New York: Holt, Rinehart & Winston.

Pauk, W. (1974). *How to study in college.* (2nd ed.). Boston: Houghton Mifflin.

Sternberg, R. J. *Writing the psychology paper.* (1977). Woodbury, NY: Barron's Educational Series.

Turabian, K. L. (1976). *Student's guide for writing college papers* (3rd ed.). Chicago: University of Chicago Press.

Wood, G. (1981). *Fundamentals of psychological research* (3rd ed.). Boston: Little, Brown.

2 Selecting and Defining the Topic

Sources Discussed
Textbooks
Handbooks
Annual Reviews

Writing a paper should be a personally rewarding learning experience. It should involve your learning about the subject, gaining information, evaluating ideas, and examining issues. It should also aid your personal growth and improve your work habits. The final product should give you a sense of accomplishment. In addition, the paper will be read by someone else—a professor, a thesis advisor, or a journal reviewer—who will evaluate it. You will learn through this evaluation process by receiving positive comments as well as feedback for improvement. Achieving both personal and academic success in writing papers requires that you master each step of the writing process while avoiding a number of pitfalls.

Importance of Selecting and Defining a Topic

The first step in a research project is selecting, narrowing, and defining a topic. Success at this stage is essential for a paper of superior quality. Although at times you may have little latitude because the topic has been assigned, at other times you may have few constraints other than paper length. In the latter case, you may find selecting a topic to be a difficult task. The topic you select should be interesting, manageable, and appropriate. Although we cannot tell you what topic to select, in this chapter we will discuss some common mistakes that students make, and we will present some rules of thumb for selecting, narrowing, and defining the topic.

Pitfalls To Avoid

Numerous mistakes are possible in writing a paper. Some of the problems listed below have been noted by other authors (e.g., Kennedy, 1979; Pauk, 1974; Sternberg, 1977; Turabian, 1976); others are observations we have made. By being aware of these problems, you may be able to avoid them.

Topic too broad. A common mistake is writing a paper on a topic that is too broad. Although a textbook may cover topics such as stress, projective personality tests, conflict, or visual illusions in a few pages and refer to only a few studies, numerous entire books have also been written about each of these topics. You probably do not plan to write a book, so you will have to limit the topic. One way to limit the paper is to set a time and a page restriction. Other ways of limiting topics are presented later in this chapter. Unless the topic is well defined, you risk writing a paper that is superficial, poorly organized, biased, or all three. Narrow your topic!

Abulia. *Webster's Dictionary* defines abulia as an "abnormal lack of ability to act or make decisions." Students have several common sources of abulia: **(a) Everything appears to be so interesting that selecting one topic seems impossible.** If you find yourself in this situation, select several interesting topics, assign a number from 1 to 6 to each one, and roll a die. If the decision of chance is not acceptable, then you really do have a preference. What is it? **(b) Nothing looks interesting enough for a paper.** If you feel this way, ask yourself why you enrolled in the course. Did you find something interesting at the beginning? If the course is required, ask yourself what about the course is so important that it is considered essential. **(c) You may feel too poorly informed to select a good paper topic.** Then start skimming the textbook, reading in greater detail sections that are interesting, and finding other sources on the topic. Set a deadline for selecting a topic!

Procrastination. Library research takes time, and there are few short cuts. Procrastination lessens your ability to be successful by limiting your time and dictating concessions in quality. Alsip and Chezik (1974) review four typical excuses students give for delaying: (a) "I don't have enough time now," (b) "I'm in the wrong place—it's too noisy or too quiet, etc.," (c) "Other things are more important," and (d) "I'm not in the right mood." Some aspects of library research—especially getting started and selecting a topic—can be accomplished by a series of small actions and in a series of small time-blocks. For example, finding a relevant book or copying a review article to get started takes only a few minutes in most college libraries. Stop wasting time!

Uninteresting topic. You will find maintaining your motivation for a project over a long period of time extremely difficult if you have little enthusiasm when you initiate the project. If you have little interest in a topic, you may be tempted to throw the paper together at the last minute. Such a paper will probably be disorganized, superficial, poorly documented, poorly typed, and unproofread; it will not only be a waste of time, it might also bring a negative reaction from the reader. Start early, explore several alternative topics, then select a topic that can sustain your interest through the ups and downs of research. Pick a topic that interests you!

Inadequate background. Some topics demand extensive knowledge of mathematics, biology, pharmacology, and so forth. Ask yourself the following questions. Do you have the background in the topic area selected to enable you to read and understand the literature on that topic? If not, will you gain the background as the course progresses, or will you have to study it independently? Do you have the time to spend in such independent study? Assess your own background to determine whether you can handle the topic.

Topic too familiar. Sternberg (1977) comments that "the purpose of student papers is for the student to learn something about some topic. It is, therefore, to the student's advantage to select a topic with which he or she is relatively unfamiliar. Students sometimes seek to optimize safety (or grades) rather than learning, however, choosing a topic with which they are quite familiar" (p. 20). Although selecting an unfamiliar area may result in a more difficult task, some professors react negatively to the practice of writing papers on the same topic for different courses and assume that the student who does so is attempting to slide by with a minimum of effort. Other professors argue that students who do this are cheating themselves by not seeking a broad education. Thus the personal and academic achievement of writing on a topic already too familiar is suspect. Select a topic about which you can learn something new!

Impressing the professor. Writing a paper is a way to integrate, evaluate, and organize your learning and to communicate it to another person. Examine your motives for selecting the topic. Attempting to destroy a theory or to impress the professor with your brilliance may backfire. You will not have time to read enough material to write an earth-shattering paper. Therefore, select a topic about which you yourself wish to learn.

Controversial topic. The goal of most courses in psychology is cognitive or affective growth or both. When dealing with controversy you may be tempted to find and to use uncritically sources that support your own point of view. Yet, as you become more involved with research, you will find that most topics are far more complex than you initially imagined. Such a discovery may lead to self-examination of your values and behaviors. The discovery of complexity, mixed with self-evaluation, may markedly increase the difficulty of your task. It may result in a positive experience if it leads to a paper of superior quality. It may, however, result in a negative experience if the complexity of the topic or your emotional involvement interferes with your completing the project. Turabian (1976) cautions that a controversial topic demands extreme care. The case must be stated clearly and precisely and must be heavily supported with documentation. Unless you have an open mind and a commitment to do thorough work, you would be advised to avoid highly controversial topics.

Resources unavailable. Often the statement, "There's nothing on my topic in the library," results from a student's inability to locate available material. There are, however, some areas in which very little has been written. For example, we have been interested in the use and effectiveness of letters of reference. If you were to research this topic, you would find that amazingly, given the widespread use of reference letters in employment situations, relatively little systematic research has been done on this topic. When selecting your topic, make sure there is enough information to write a good paper.

Reliance on secondary sources. Some students find two or three books and proceed to write a paper based on these sources. This activity is not research; it is book reporting. In general, books are secondary sources, summarizing, interpreting, evaluating, and reporting the research and theorizing of others. Although books are usually accurate, an author may inaccurately report or may exclude an important piece of research because of misinterpretation, prejudice, misjudgment, or sloppy scholarship. Several recent articles (e.g., Bramel & Friend, 1981; Hogan & Schroeder, 1981; Samelson, 1974) have commented on the apparent inaccuracies in a number of authoritative, standard sources. Unless you read the original source, you cannot be certain that your reporting and evaluation are accurate.

Guidelines for Selecting a Topic

Having recounted a list of potential problems and situations to avoid, we now offer positive suggestions for selecting a topic. You should select a topic that meets the following criteria:

- **Interesting:** The topic should be something about which you want to learn.

- **Appropriate:** The topic should be directly relevant to your situation. You should have the background and knowledge to be able to read and understand the materials you will encounter.

- **Manageable:** The topic must be sufficiently limited so that you can do a credible job in the time and space available. You will probably need to restrict your topic several times after selecting an initial topic area.

- **Researchable:** The topic should be feasible given the resources available to you.

For other discussions of topic selection, consult such sources as Campbell and Ballou (1978), Pauk (1974), Sternberg (1977), or Turabian (1976).

Defining the Topic

A clear, concise topic definition is essential for an effective literature search. Such a definition will provide guidelines for evaluating materials and determining their relevance or irrelevance. After spending hours of reading and taking notes on material for your paper, you may be tempted to include unessential information in the paper. Such inclusion may result in a disorganized, poorly focused paper. You can minimize this temptation by effectively defining your topic.

Campbell and Ballou (1978) suggest two ways of expressing a topic: (a) as a thesis statement or (b) as a question. For example, the following might be acceptable ways of initially defining a topic concerning occupational stress.

Thesis statement: Occupational stress has a negative effect on interpersonal relations and thus adversely affects job performance in managerial workers.

Question: What is the effect of occupational stress on managerial job performance in situations concerning interpersonal relations?

Either of these ways of expressing the topic might be an acceptable form in your situation. Both of these topic sentences, however, are still fairly broad. What kinds of interpersonal relations—peer relations, supervisor-subordinate relations, and so on—and what kind of job performance will you consider? Exactly what do you mean by occupational stress? Thus you must take the next step and narrow the topic to a more manageable size.

Limiting the Topic

You can narrow a topic several times in several ways. Pauk (1974) suggests that every topic be subjected to three or four significant narrowings to reach a topic of manageable size. The following list, based in part on suggestions of Sternberg (1977), shows a number of dimensions along which a topic may be limited.

Subject population. Age limitation: You may be interested only in a particular age group, for example, infants, adolescents, college students, or retirees. Occupational group limitation: You may be interested only in middle managers, blue-collar workers, secretaries, or military personnel. Racial or ethnic limitation: You may be interested, for example, only in black, native, Spanish-speaking, or Asian Americans.

Theoretical approach. You might limit a clinically oriented study to a behavior-modification approach, a Gestalt approach, or a psychodynamic approach. For a study in human judgment you might select from among a Bayesian, an information-integration, or a policy-capturing approach.

Species restriction. In a learning, comparative, physiological, or ethological study, you might focus your interest on rats, pigeons, chimpanzees, cats, dogs, eels, chickens, or humans.

Research methodology employed. You might limit consideration to only laboratory studies, simulations, field experiments, surveys, interviews, or naturalistic observation. Your reporting might concentrate on studies that involve deception or on those that do not involve deception, on studies that involve a particular piece of psychological equipment, or on studies that employ a particular psychological test.

Content of problem. In an information-processing topic, you might consider only studies of numerical information, those of verbal information, or those of pictorial information. Or you might limit the number of examples and treat these in depth. In a study of perceptual illusions, for example, you might limit yourself to one or two particular illusions.

Limiting a topic depends upon your purpose in writing the paper and upon the area you wish to cover. You might need to limit two different topics in entirely different fashions for different reasons. The way you limit a topic ultimately depends upon making good judgments. But how and where do you begin?

Sources To Get Started

After you have selected and defined a general topic, you are ready to begin the process of narrowing. A good way to figure out how to narrow your topic is to consult several types of general sources to get a feel for the area, an overview of the topic, and a number of subareas or subtopics from which to select. These general sources should also provide relevant and major references for beginning your search. This section discusses three types of general sources: (a) textbooks, (b) handbooks, and (c) annual reviews. To illustrate the use of these sources, we have selected three different topics and will narrow each topic using one of the three sources.

Textbooks

You might begin with your textbook, reading material relevant to your topic several times. This material may span an entire chapter (a hint that the topic is broad and requires considerable limiting) or the material may be covered in a paragraph or two. Check the sources that are cited. Every good textbook should refer to important, relevant sources, providing complete bibliographic information, for all major topics covered. With those references, you can start a literature search, using the references provided in those sources to find other materials. If, however, the topic that interests you is not mentioned in your textbook, find another recent textbook that does cover the topic. In the course of gathering this information, you will find phrases that will help you in limiting your topic.

To illustrate topic limitation, we consider a topic popular in developmental psychology, Piaget's theory of child development. In their textbook, *Child Psychology: A Contemporary Viewpoint*, Hetherington and Parke (1979) discuss Piaget's theory in chapters 8, 9, and 16. The discussion in three chapters as well as references to four books by Piaget indicate that his theory of child development is a large topic. Chapter 9, however, covers a more limited area: "Piaget's Cognitive Developmental Theory of Intelligence." Within that chapter, pages 320 to 325 cover the intuitive period (age 4—7) of a child's development. Although this topic is narrower, we still have

TABLE 2—A

Sequential Steps in Limiting a Topic in Developmental Psychology

Stage	Topic Statement
Initial topic	Piaget's theory of child development
1st narrowing	Piaget's cognitive developmental theory of intelligence
2nd narrowing	Cognitive development in the intuitive period
3rd narrowing	Conservation in the intuitive period
4th narrowing	Conservation of number in the intuitive period
5th narrowing	Training conservation in the intuitive period
Final statement	Effectiveness of attempts to stimulate cognitive development in intuitive-period children (age 4–7) through training conservation

much to consider: problems of conservation, transformations, centration, irreversibility, and part-whole relations. Looking at the illustrations, we see that Figure 9–3 mentions tests for conservation of substance, length, number, liquids, and area.

If you were working on this topic, you might, at this point, limit the topic to conservation of number. You might focus on the statement on page 325 that some researchers have wondered whether training children in conservation strategies can stimulate cognitive growth in other areas. You then might settle on the topic of the "effectiveness of attempts to stimulate cognitive growth in intuitive-period children through training conservation." You have now narrowed your topic by selecting a specific subject population (intuitive-age children), theoretical approach (Piagetian conception of conservation), and problem content (effect of conservation training on other areas of learning). This topic narrowing is summarized in Table 2–A. Finally, the textbook provides several relevant references, which give you a direction in which to start your library research.

Handbooks

If you have already decided on an area you wish to study, you will find a logical second place to begin is with a handbook. Most handbooks have several characteristics that make them especially well suited for narrowing a topic and beginning a literature search.
- They provide an authoritative summary of a particular area, including evaluations of theory and research.
- They are written by experts in the field. Although one person sometimes writes a handbook, more commonly one person edits the contributions of a large number of authors, each of whom writes in his or her special area of interest and expertise.
- They are usually written at a level for a beginning graduate student in the particular subfield and are more comprehensive than most textbooks.

TABLE 2–B

Sequential Steps in Limiting a Topic in Social Psychology: Psychology of Women

Stage	Topic Statement
Initial topic	Women as leaders
1st narrowing	Women's success as leaders
Final statement	Attributes of successful women managers

• They contain extensive reference lists.

Be aware, however, that not all subfields of psychology are covered by recent handbooks. In some areas, such as brain biochemistry, human factors in display-control design, and information processing, handbooks can become obsolete very rapidly.

The use of one handbook is illustrated in this section. At the end of chapter 2, you will find a selected list of handbooks that might help you begin.

Suppose your topic is women as leaders, a contemporary concern in social psychology, organizational psychology, and psychology of women. One logical starting point is *Stogdill's Handbook of Leadership* (Bass, 1981). When you examine the table of contents (or the subject index), you see that chapter 30, "Women and Leadership," appears to be useful. This 17-page chapter contains references to approximately 200 sources. It also divides the topic of women and leadership into six major areas: societal conditions, male-female differences in leadership potential, male-female differences in leadership style, sex effects contingent on groups and situations, women's success as leaders, and the effectiveness of women leaders. Although you could use these divisions to narrow the topic—you could, for example, pick "women's success as leaders" (section 5)—you would be advised to limit the topic still further because of the large amount of information available. Part two of section 5 covers the "attributes of the successful woman manager," which seems to be a good possibility for research. This section contains 14 references, most of which are fairly recent. At the outset, then, the topic appears to be reasonably limited, with some relevant resources. Thus you have limited this topic by your own interest, by subject population (women, managers), and by content of the problem (effective managers). The successive topic limiting may be seen more easily in Table 2–B.

Annual Reviews

A third important source of information for defining and limiting a topic is the *Annual Review of Psychology.* The first volume, containing 18 review articles, appeared in 1950. Since then, the annual volumes have included from 15 to 22 articles each year. In recent years, as the field of psychology has expanded, reviews have become more focused and specialized, and new topics have been added. The plan of the *Annual Review* is well summarized in the preface to Volume 32 (1981):

Each volume is planned to present selective and evaluative re-

TABLE 2—C

Sequential Steps in Limiting a Topic in Physiological Psychology

Stage	Topic Statement
Initial topic	Self-stimulation of the brain
1st narrowing	Physiological pathways supporting self-stimulation
2nd narrowing	Neurochemical aspects of reward pathways in intracranial self-stimulation
Final statement	Role of opiate receptors and endorphins in intracranial self-stimulation

views of status and recent progress in several main areas of psychology. We do not intend to provide in a single volume an accurate representation of activity in each of the many subfields of psychology; space would not permit this. Rather, we try to follow (and frequently revise) a Master Plan according to which some topics appear each year, some every other year, and some less frequently. In this way, a few successive volumes, taken together, present an evaluative portrayal of the main recent findings and interpretations as they are viewed by the most expert judges who can be persuaded to contribute their critical and integrative skills to the task.[1]

A sampling of recent topics includes the following: human learning, child psychopathology, attitudes and attitude change, visual neural development, instructional psychology, animal cognition, brain functions, group therapy, organizational behavior, consumer psychology, event perception, social motivation, the school as a social situation, spatial vision, and sleep and dreams.

For illustrative purposes, suppose you are interested in self-stimulation of the brain, the finding that eliciting behavior that normally occurs with natural rewards is possible through direct stimulation of the brain. Volume 32 of the *Annual Review of Psychology* contains a review of this area (Olds & Fobes, 1981). Examining this review, you find references to research that has concentrated on physiological pathways supporting self-stimulation. You might limit your topic to the neurochemical aspects of those reward pathways. Then you might find most interesting the section on the role of opiate receptors and endorphins in self-stimulation (covered on pp. 563–564). Here again, you find a number of relevant references. You have narrowed this topic by attending to a particular research methodology (direct self-stimulation of the brain) and problem content (the role of particular chemicals in brain stimulation). The steps in narrowing this topic are summarized in Table 2—C. Two notes of caution are important here. First, this field is expanding so rapidly that you may need to narrow the topic still further. Second,

---

[1]From Preface by M. R. Rosenzweig & L. W. Porter (Eds.), 1981, *Annual Review of Psychology*, *32*, p. v. Copyright © 1981 by Annual Reviews Inc. Reprinted by permission.

this topic is extremely complex and demands extensive knowledge of physiology and brain biochemistry.

Nothing should prevent your use of all three of these types of sources. Because each source is selective, presenting only a few of the many available resources, you can expect each to contain a slightly different group of primary source materials. Furthermore, because the sources are written by different authors, they express different points of view.

Selecting Subject-Search Terms

The final preliminary step in doing library research is developing a set of subject terms to be used to search for information. When beginning research in a new area, students often search for information by subject. And most sources, including all of the sources discussed in the following chapters, contain subject indexes. However, indexes are compiled by different people, some by psychologists and others by persons having little detailed knowledge of psychology. As a result, the index of each source will be different and may use a different set of subject-indexing terms.

Determining in advance how a particular topic will be indexed is difficult. For example, in the sample topic on leadership, you might find that some sources list information only under *women managers* whereas others use only the term *female managers.* Sources may include research under one of the terms *leadership, supervision,* or *management* but not under all three. Because of the complexity of the subject of personality, terms used to describe a successful woman manager might be *characteristics, attributes, traits,* or *styles.*

As a result, you must compile a list of subject-search terms that you could use to locate relevant information on a topic. You should include in this list any synonyms, technical terms, or important aspects of the topic of interest. Later, as you use particular sources, you may modify the list of search terms to match the subject-indexing terms of each source.

Table 2–D contains sample lists of search terms for the three topics illustrated in this chapter. Each list is different in the number of terms, the technicality of terms, and the number of synonyms. In every search, these differences will reflect the particular character of the research topic.

Summary Steps in Defining a Topic

The following is a brief review of six general steps in getting started. A different sequence may better suit your style, but at some point, each process requires attention.
• Select a general topic, being as specific as possible.
• Define the topic as a statement or as a question.
• Get an overview of the topic by reading the textbook, a handbook, an annual review chapter, or all three.
• Limit the topic to a manageable size.
• Redefine the narrowed topic.
• Devise a list of possible search terms.
You are now ready to start consulting the primary sources you have

TABLE 2–D

Initial Lists of Search Terms for Sample Topics

Topic	Search Terms	
Training Conservation in Children	conservation (psychology) intuitive period child intelligence Piaget	cognitive development child development teaching conservation
Successful Women Leaders	women females managers leaders supervisors	characteristics traits attributes styles
Self-Stimulation of the Brain	self-stimulation brain stimulation neural stimulation	opiate receptors endorphins neurochemistry

already located and to begin searching for additional relevant references.

Selected Handbooks

This list of handbooks is intended to be illustrative rather than exhaustive. The sources are grouped by general area. All of the handbooks mentioned here contain extensive lists of references. A few handbooks are a bit old, and, to the extent that they cover rapidly changing fields, you must use them with care.

General Sources

Kling, J. W., et al. (1971). *Woodworth and Schlossberg's experimental psychology* (3rd ed.). New York: Holt, Rinehart & Winston.

Twenty-one chapters, 1100 pages, 100-page bibliography. This classic, written by 19 expert researchers, is geared toward the advanced undergraduate or first-year graduate student. It is a complete revision of earlier editions published in 1938 and 1954. Although it is intended to be a textbook, its authoritativeness and comprehensiveness make it usable as a handbook. It covers such topics as psychophysics; chemical senses; color vision; and transfer, inference, and forgetting.

Stevens, S. S. (Ed.). (1951). *Handbook of experimental psychology.* New York: Wiley.

Thirty-six chapters, 1360 pages. This classic is one of the earliest attempts to summarize the field in a multiple-author handbook. It is especially well known for chapter 1 (on measurement) written by Stevens.

Wolman, B. B. (Ed.). (1973). *Handbook of general psychology.* Englewood Cliffs, NJ: Prentice-Hall.

Forty-five chapters, 950+ pages, multiple authors. Chapters include "Theories of Intelligence" by J. P. Guilford, "Theories of Motivation" by K. B. Madsen, and "Structured Personality Assessment" by D. N. Jackson.

Learning, Motivation, Sensory Processes

Carterette, E. C., & Friedman, M. (Eds.). (1973–1978). *Handbook of perception* (10 vols.). New York: Academic Press.

Ten volumes, multiple authors. Volumes include the following: *I. Historical and philosophical roots of perception; III. Biology of perceptual systems; V. Seeing; X. Perceptual ecology.*

Psychology of learning and motivation: Advances in research and theory. (1967–present, Vols. 1+). New York: Academic Press.

Published annually, multiple authors. This handbook may be seen as a companion to the *Annual Review of Psychology*, with a narrower range of topics.

University of Nebraska, Department of Psychology. (1953–present). *Current theory and research in motivation, a symposium.* (Vols. 1+) Lincoln, NE: University of Nebraska Press.

Commonly known as *Nebraska Symposium on Motivation;* published annually. Strictly speaking, this is not a handbook; however, important articles represent the state of the art at the time of their publication. For example, the inaugural volume contained chapters by J. S. Brown, H. F. Harlow, L. J. Postman, V. Nowlis, T. M. Newcomb, and O. H. Mowrer. For many years, this symposium has played a key role in the development of motivational psychology.

Developmental, Personality, Social

Abelson, R. P., Aronson, E., McGuire, W. J., Newcomb, T. M., Rosenberg, M. J., & Tannenbaum, P. H. (Eds.). (1968). *Theories of cognitive consistency: A sourcebook.* Chicago: Rand McNally.

Eighty-four chapters, 800+ pages. Approaches covered include balance theory (F. Heider), conflict theory (K. Lewin), dissonance theory (L. Festinger), and congruity theory (C. E. Osgood & P. M. Tannenbaum). Although dated, the book provides an excellent review of cognitive consistency theories.

Borgatta, E. F., & Lamberg, W. W. (Eds.). (1968). *Handbook of personality theory and research.* Chicago: Rand McNally.

Twenty-four chapters, 1100 pages, multiple authors, dated.

Knutson, J. N. (Ed.). (1973). *Handbook of political psychology.* San Francisco: Jossey-Bass.

Sixteen chapters, including "Political Attitudes," "Political Socialization," and "Experimental Research."

Lindzey, G., & Aronson, E. (Eds.). (1968). *The handbook of social psychology* (2nd ed.). Reading, MA: Addison-Wesley.

Five volumes, 45 chapters, 68 authors. A classic and excellent reference.

Mussen, P. H. (Ed.). (1983). *Carmichael's manual of child psychology* (4th ed.). New York: Wiley.

Four volumes, 47 chapters, more than 75 contributing authors. Volumes: *I. History, theory and methods* (W. Kessen, Ed.); *II. Infancy and developmental psychobiology* (J. Campos & M. Haith, Eds.); *III. Cognitive development* (J. Flavell & E. Markman, Eds.); *IV. Socialization, personality and social development* (E. M. Hetherington, Ed.).

Osofsky, J. D. (Ed.). (1979). *Handbook of infant development*. New York: Wiley.
> Twenty-eight chapters, 44 contributing authors, 900 pages. Chapters include "Early Infant Assessment," "Learning in Infancy," "Infant Visual Perception," "Parent-Infant Bonding," and "Effects of Maternal Drinking."

Operant Behavior

Gambrill, E. D. (1977). *Behavior modification: A handbook of assessment, intervention and evaluation*. San Francisco: Jossey-Bass.
> Twenty-three chapters, 1000+ pages. Chapters include "Assessment," "Intervention Plans," "Anxiety Reduction," "Drug Abuse," "Depression," "Educational Settings," and "Ethics."

Honig, W. K., & Staddon, J. E. R. (Eds.). (1977). *Handbook of operant behavior*. Englewood Cliffs, NJ: Prentice-Hall.

Progress in behavior modification. (1975—present, Vols. 1+). New York: Academic Press.
> Two volumes published annually, multiple authors. The preface describes this handbook as a "multidisciplinary serial publication encompassing the contributions of psychology, psychiatry, social work, speech therapy, education, and rehabilitation."

Clinical, Counseling, Industrial-Organizational

Dunnette, M. D. (Ed.). (1976). *Handbook of industrial and organizational psychology*. Chicago: Rand McNally.
> Multiple authors, 1500 pages. Chapters include "Motivation Theory in I/O Psychology," "Field Research Methods," "Problem of Criteria," "Psychometric Theory," and "Nature and Causes of Job Satisfaction."

Rie, H. E., & Rie, E. D. (Eds.). (1980). *Handbook of minimal brain dysfunctions: A critical view*. New York: Wiley.
> Twenty-seven chapters, 31 contributors, rather specialized. Chapters include "Concept of MBD," "Determinants of MBD," "Evaluation of MBD," and "Intervention."

Struening, E. L., & Guttentag, M. (Eds.). (1975). *Handbook of evaluation research*. Beverly Hills, CA: Sage.
> Two volumes. Chapters cover a range of issues, including those of political influences, design of evaluation studies, and data analysis.

Woody, R. H. (Ed.). (1980). *Encyclopedia of clinical assessment*. San Francisco: Jossey-Bass.
> Two volumes, 91 chapters, 110 authors. Chapters include "Academic Learning Problems," "Affective Guilt States," "Aggression," "Altruism," "Ambiguity Tolerance," and "Antisocial Personality."

References

Alsip, J. E., & Chezik, D. D. (1974). *Research guide in psychology*. Morristown, NJ: General Learning Press.

Bass, B. M. (1981). *Stogdill's handbook of leadership: A survey of theory and research* (2nd ed.). New York: Free Press.

Bramel, D., & Friend, R. (1981). Hawthorne, the myth of the docile worker, and class bias in psychology. *American Psychologist, 36,* 867–878.

Campbell, W. G., & Ballou, S. W. (1978). *Form and style: Theses, reports, term papers* (5th ed.). Boston: Houghton Mifflin.

Hetherington, E. M., & Parke, R. D. (1979). *Child psychology: A contemporary viewpoint* (2nd ed.). New York: McGraw-Hill.

Hogan, R., & Schroeder, D. (1981, July). Critique: Seven biases in psychology. *Psychology Today,* pp. 8–14.

Kennedy, J. R. (1979). *Library research guide to education: Illustrated search strategies and sources.* Ann Arbor, MI: Pierian Press.

Olds, M. E., & Fobes, J. L. (1981). The central basis of motivation: Intracranial self-stimulation studies. *Annual Review of Psychology, 32,* 523–574.

Pauk, W. (1974). *How to study in college* (2nd ed.). Boston: Houghton Mifflin.

Samelson, F. (1974). History, origin myth and ideology: "Discovery" of social psychology. *Journal for the Theory of Social Behavior, 4,* 217–231.

Sternberg, R. J. (1977). *Writing the psychology paper.* Woodbury, NY: Barron's Educational Series.

Turabian, K. L. (1976). *Student's guide for writing college papers* (3rd ed.). Chicago: University of Chicago Press.

3 Locating a Book

Sources Discussed
Library Card Catalog
Library of Congress, Subject Cataloging Division. (1980). *Library of Congress subject headings* (9th ed.). Washington, DC: Library of Congress.

This chapter presents procedures for identifying and locating monographs (books) in the library. Monographs appear in many formats: single-volume books (e.g., *Library Use*), multiple-volume sets (e.g., *Handbook of Perception*), annual series (e.g., *Annual Review of Psychology*), and so forth. They may contain reviews of literature and extensive bibliographies. Some books contain important new theoretical approaches; others contain original empirical contributions. However, books may be limited in several ways. They may present only one author's point of view or only his or her research. Writing and publishing a book is a complicated, time-consuming process; thus, a book may not contain the most recent research. Hence, although books may provide important background for your literature review, they should be only part of your research. You will also need to locate journals (discussed in chapters 4, 5, and 6) in which most research reports are published.

This chapter discusses the card catalog, an index to monographs contained in a library. The chapter first focuses on a sample topic, then discusses the organization of the card catalog and ways of using it, and concludes with a discussion of subject-indexing terms.

Chapter Example: Intelligence and Heredity

In this chapter we use the topic of intelligence, more specifically, hereditary influences on intelligence, to illustrate the search for monographs. Although much has been written on this issue, we leave the topic somewhat broad for the purpose of illustration. Also, we have selected this controversial topic (contrary to our advice contained in chapter 2) in order to illustrate how complex a controversial topic may be and how much material may be available in an area. To write a good paper in this area, however, you would have to limit the topic severely.

Several important themes and questions are involved in this topic. What is intelligence? Do IQ tests measure intelligence? To what extent is one's intelligence determined by heredity, the genes with which one is born (nature)? To what extent is intelligence influenced by the environment in which one is born, grows, and lives (nurture)? Are children who are raised in a culturally, economically, nutritionally, or educationally deprived environment likely to have lower intelligence? Are some racial groups inherently less intelligent than others? Can intelligence or IQ test scores be changed? Is compensatory education a feasible method for improving the intelligence of disadvantaged children?

Many of these questions have been discussed in the recent history of the United States. In the 1960s programs were initiated to provide compensatory education to disadvantaged children (U.S. Dept. of Health & Human Services, 1980). In 1969 Arthur Jensen questioned the value of compensatory education programs in an article titled "How Much Can We Boost IQ and Scholastic Achievement?" citing early evaluations of the Head Start Project, which found no long-term gains in the IQs of disadvantaged children. He noted that, on the average, black children have lower IQs than white children. Discussing the extent to which intelligence is environmentally, as opposed to genetically, influenced, he concluded that the primary contributor to intelligence is heredity (Jensen, 1969, 1972). These arguments and early evaluations of the Head Start Project subsequently appeared in public-policy discussions of compensatory-education programs and their funding (e.g., see Brazziel, 1969; Nixon, 1971; Spicker, 1969; U.S. Senate, 1972). In response to Jensen's article, much controversy arose concerning what IQ tests measure, whether they are inherently biased, and whether the studies on which Jensen was relying had been adequately conducted (e.g., Bodmer & Cavalli-Sforza, 1970; Cronbach, 1975; Haney, 1981; Herrnstein, 1971, 1982; McCall, 1970; Rowan, 1970). One influential book in this controversy was *The Science and Politics of I.Q.* by Leon J. Kamin (1974), a professor at Princeton.

Card Catalog

With this brief background, we can begin to identify sources that are involved with the controversy over the nature of intelligence and of IQ tests, by locating Kamin's book in the library. Every library uses some system to organize its hundreds of thousands of books. Most libraries arrange books on the shelves by codes known as call numbers, which are printed on the spine (bound end) of the book. To

TABLE 3—A

Alphabetical Orderings of Selected Authors, Titles, and Subjects of Books

Author	Title	Subject
Adorno, T. W.	*Basic behavioral statistics*	emotions
Allport, G. W.	*Behavior and psychological man*	environment
Anastasi, A.	*Behavior therapy*	evolution
Anderson, N. H.	*The behavioral sciences today*	experiments
Aronson, E.	*Being mentally ill*	fantasy
Bandura, A.	*Beyond burnout*	fear

find the number of Kamin's book, we need to use an index to those call numbers. For most libraries, that index is the card catalog.

You are probably familiar with three basic types of indexes. In author indexes information is arranged in alphabetical order by the last name of the person who wrote a book or paper. In title indexes material is arranged alphabetically by title. In subject indexes, books are listed alphabetically by general topic and, within the general topic, alphabetically by subtopic. Table 3—A illustrates each of these types of indexes. Card catalogs contain entries of all three types for each book in the library. Some libraries group all three types of indexes together in a single alphabetical order (a dictionary catalog). Other libraries separate the different types of index entries (divided catalogs); for example, a library may have one catalog combining the author and title indexes (author/title catalog) and a separate catalog that contains the subject index (subject catalog).

When looking for a book by a particular author, you must start with the author catalog. With the topic selected for illustration, you would therefore start by searching for "Kamin, Leon J." Cards in the catalog are filed alphabetically by the top line of each card, in this case, by the author's last name (surname), then by the first name if more than one person has the same last name. If the top lines of several cards are identical (indicating several books by the same author), cards are ordered alphabetically by the second line, which usually indicates a book title.[1] Each catalog card provides the same

---

[1] There are numerous exceptions to general rules regarding libraries; the catalog contains many. Four common problems are illustrated here. Although APA publication style uses the author's first and middle initials in references, most libraries make entries under the author's full name, if it is known. Thus a book by Adam Smith would be cited as "Smith, A." in an APA publication; it would be filed in the card catalog under "Smith, Adam." This distinction is particularly important with authors who have common surnames, for example, Johnson, Jones, or Smith.

In many libraries, names beginning with M', Mc, and Mac are ordered together as if all were spelled "Mac." The following list illustrates card catalog ordering of several names: MacBride, McDowell, MacGregor, M'Intosh, Mack, Macmillan, McShane.

Separate entries may be made for an author and a subject that appear to be the same. For example, books by Freud would appear in the author catalog under "Freud, Sigmund." Books about him or about his writings would be entered in the subject catalog (or, in a combined catalog, after all books written by him) under the all-uppercase subject heading FREUD, SIGMUND.

If a book title begins with an article (i.e., *a, an,* or *the*), librarians overlook this article when alphabetizing titles in the card catalog. For example, *The Origin of Species* would be filed alphabetically under "Origin of species."

FIGURE 3–A

Card-catalog author (main entry) cards for Leon J. Kamin's (1974) *The Science and Politics of I.Q.*, illustrating the use of both Library of Congress (LC) and Dewey Decimal call numbers.

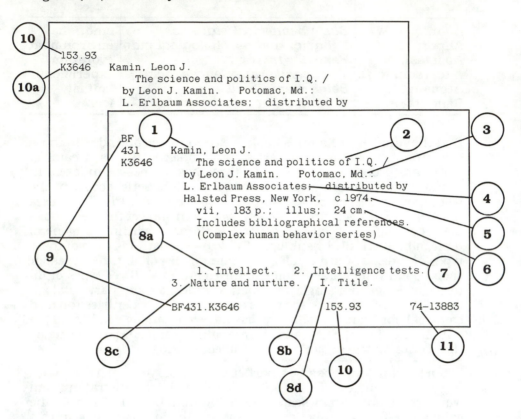

types of information about books in the same relative position on the card.

When you go to the catalog, you should find a card that looks like the picture of the 3″ x 5″ catalog card in Figure 3–A. In that figure, the author, Leon J. Kamin, is listed at the top of the card (**1**), and the rest of the bibliographic information follows. The title of Kamin's book is *The Science and Politics of I.Q.* (**2**). The book was published in Potomac, Maryland, (**3**) by Lawrence Erlbaum Associates, (**4**) and was distributed by Halsted Press, which is located in New York City. It was copyrighted in 1974, the year of its publication (**5**). The lines that follow provide a physical description of the book (**6**): The book has 7 prefatory pages and 183 pages of text, contains illustrations, is approximately 24 centimeters (9.6 inches) tall, and includes a bibliography. It is part of the "Complex Human Behavior" series of publications by Erlbaum (**7**).

Below the descriptive information on the card is the **tracing** (**8**), which informs the librarian and the library user how this particular book has been further indexed in the card catalog. The tracing is designed by a cataloging librarian who examines the book, learns what topics it covers, and assigns terms known as **subject headings** to describe the book's contents.

Three subject headings have been assigned to Kamin's book. Indicated by Arabic numbers, they are: **Intellect (8a)**, **Intelligence tests (8b)**, and **Nature and nurture (8c)**. If your library has a divided catalog, these subject headings would be found in the subject catalog. Additionally, there is a tracing for the title of the book (**8d**) after the Roman numeral "I." Thus you would find cards in five places in the catalog: listed alphabetically under the author's name, under the book title, and under each of the three subject headings. The entry cards for tracings, as they would appear in most catalogs, are illustrated in Figure 3–B. Note that each card is the same as the author card (the main entry), except that the tracing that provides the index entry location is typed at the top of the card.

FIGURE 3–B
Catalog cards for tracings (i.e., subject headings and title entry), noted in Figure 3–A, for *The Science and Politics of I.Q.*

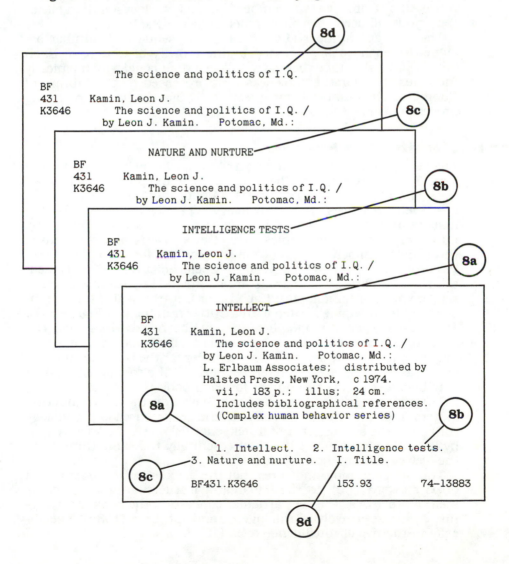

The bottom line of the card represented in Figure 3—A contains three numbers. The first number is the Library of Congress classification number (9); the second is the Dewey Decimal classification number (10); the third is the Library of Congress card number (11). As previously mentioned, most libraries in the United States arrange books on the shelves by call number.

In most libraries the classification number is used as the call number. Libraries using the Library of Congress (LC) system type the LC number (9) in the upper left corner of each card; libraries using the Dewey Decimal system place the Dewey number (10) in the upper left corner of each card (see Figure 3—A). Because many libraries purchase printed cards and may modify the class number for their particular library's needs, you should use the call number typed in the upper left corner of the card to locate the book. In most college libraries, you will be able to go directly to the bookshelves and find the book. In some larger research libraries, however, users are required to place written requests for books that are located and retrieved by a library staff member (a closed-stack system). In either case, you will need the call number to locate the book.

The LC card number (11) is a unique, sequential number assigned to each book processed by the Library of Congress. Each book's LC card number begins with a two-digit code, which typically indicates the year the book was first processed by the Library of Congress. The number is most frequently used by librarians in the process of cataloging books.

Classification Systems

The LC classification system uses a combination of letters and numbers. Each entry begins with one or two letters representing a broad class of knowledge, for example, B = Philosophy, BF = Psychology, H = Social Sciences, HM = Sociology, Q = Science, QA = Mathematics, and R = Medicine. These general areas are subdivided by numbers into smaller topics. The Dewey Decimal system uses three-digit numbers ranging from 001 to 999, for example, 100 = Philosophy, 150 = Psychology, 300 = Social Sciences, 370 = Education, and so forth. These areas are subdivided by numbers representing more specific topics. Each LC or Dewey classification number is typically supplemented with a Cutter number (see Figure 3—A, 10a), usually identifying the author of the book. Thus each call number contains two parts: The first is an indication of the book's major topic, and the second is an identifier for the book's author. In some cases, if there are different editions of the same book, a date may be added. The call number for each book is unique.

The call number for Kamin's book, based on the LC numbering system, indicates that the book is in the general area of psychology (BF), is in the specific area of intelligence (BF431), and was written by Leon Kamin (K3646). We learn essentially the same thing from the Dewey call number.

The Dewey number indicates that the book is in the general area of psychology (150), in the subarea of intellectual and conscious mental processes (153). A particular concern in the book is for cognitive processes involving intelligence and aptitudes (153.9), specifically in the use of intelligence tests (153.93).

FIGURE 3–C

Location by call number of *The Science and Politics of I.Q.* in relation to the call numbers of other possible books on the library shelf. (The order proceeds from left to right and from top line to bottom line within the call number.)

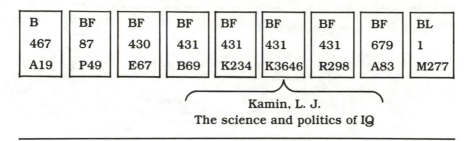

B	BF	BF	BF	BF	BF	BF	BF	BL
467	87	430	431	431	431	431	679	1
A19	P49	E67	B69	K234	K3646	R298	A83	M277

Kamin, L. J.
The science and politics of IQ

Figure 3–C shows how Kamin's book would be located by call number in relation to eight other call numbers in the LC system. The call number beginning with B comes before that beginning with BF, and numbers proceed from the smallest to the largest, 40 before 300 before 2000. Cutter numbers are read as though preceded by a decimal point, for example, the following sequence: K237, K3, K36, K3646, K4, K55.

Both the LC and Dewey systems were devised in the late 1800s. Although they have been revised continually, each contains some fundamental curiosities. In the past 100 years, knowledge has grown more in some areas than in others. In 1890, psychology was a new discipline, with its roots in philosophy and in medicine. Thus psychology was classified within the larger groups of philosophy (B in LC, 100 in Dewey) and medicine (R in LC, 610 in Dewey). Also, materials of possible interest to a psychologist may be scattered further about the library, classified with sociology, education, biology, and mathematics. This situation is illustrated in Table 3–B, which presents a sampling of important subareas within psychology and their locations within the LC and Dewey classification systems. (LC and Dewey are the most widely used book-classification systems in the United States; however, a number of others do exist, used most frequently in specialized libraries, e.g., medical or agriculture libraries.)

The problem of scatter is compounded by the fact that librarians make judgments in assigning classification numbers and subject headings. Because two persons may make different decisions, books covering several major topics, or in emerging fields, may be assigned different classification numbers. This situation can make your task as a researcher extremely difficult. Figure 3–D illustrates this problem.

We identified three books in the subject catalog using the subject heading INTELLIGENCE TESTS (8b). One, *Race and I.Q.* (12), would be found near the Kamin book with other books on intelligence within Psychology (BF) (13); another, by Scagliotta (14), would be located in class LB (15), the general field of Education; a third, by Allen (16), would be located in RC (17) with Medicine.

FIGURE 3–D

Catalog cards of monographs, showing subject headings included in the tracings of *The Science and Politics of I.Q.*

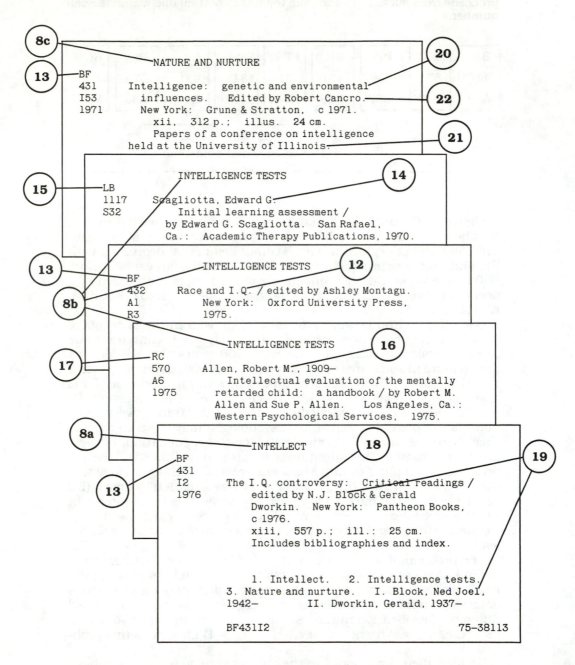

Use of Tracings

If you recall that Kamin's book was indexed under three subject headings—INTELLECT, INTELLIGENCE TESTS, and NATURE AND NURTURE (see Figures 3–A and 3–B), you can reasonably assume that other books would also be indexed under the subject headings provided by the tracing. We proceeded in our search by consulting each of these subject headings in the catalog. The subject heading INTELLECT (**8a**) yielded a book of readings (see Figure 3–D) entitled *The I.Q. Controversy* (**18**), edited by N. J. Block and Gerald Dworkin (**19**), and classified in Psychology (BF). The subject heading INTELLIGENCE TESTS (**8b**) identified the three books discussed in the previous section as well as many other books. Checking the NATURE AND NURTURE subject heading (**8c**), we located *Intelligence: Genetic and Environmental Influences* (**20**). This monograph, edited by Robert Cancro (**22**), contains papers presented at a conference at the University of Illinois (**21**).

TABLE 3–B

Distribution of Psychology-Relevant Materials Throughout the Library in the Library of Congress and Dewey Decimal Classification Systems

Library of Congress Class	Subject Area	Dewey Decimal Class
BF173 or RC554	Abnormal psychology (personality disorders)	157
Q335	Artificial intelligence	001.53
BF721	Child psychology	155.4
BF311	Cognition	153.4
BF660-687	Comparative psychology	156
LB1051-1091	Educational psychology	370.15
BF353	Environmental psychology	155.9
HQ19	Family (social groups)	306.8
HF5548.8	Industrial psychology	158.7
BF683	Motivation	153.8
BF1001-1999	Parapsychology and the occult	133
BF311	Perception	153.7
BF698	Personality	155.2
HF5549 or T56-58	Personnel management	658.3
BF181 or QP351	Physiological psychology	152
HV689	Psychiatric social work	362.2
RC336-340	Psychiatry	616.89
BF455-463	Psycholinguistics (psychology of language)	401
QA273 or BF39	Statistics (correlation), psychometrics	519.5
RC435-630	Psychotherapy	616.89
HM251-291	Social psychology	302
LC4601-4700	Special education (mentally handicapped children)	371.92
HQ1206-1216	Women, psychology of	305.4

Subject-Headings List

If we had not known of the Kamin book or another similar starting point, we would have begun the search with the subject catalog. After defining the topic, we would have listed a set of descriptive subject terms based on a topic statement (see chapter 2). The following list shows some terms with which we might begin a search: intelligence, intelligence testing, heritability, compensatory education, intelligence modification, nature and nurture.

Our next step would be to consult the list of subject headings used in the library. One of the most widely used listings is *Library of Congress Subject Headings* (9th Edition). This huge, two-volume set is shelved near the subject catalog in many libraries. (Ask a librarian to point it out if you cannot find it. If your library uses a different system of subject headings, become familiar with that one.) *Library of Congress Subject Headings* is a guide to the **controlled vocabulary** of subject-indexing terms used by the Library of Congress in cataloging books. Only authorized terms contained in the list are used as subject headings and appear as tracings on catalog cards. If a descriptive term you wish to use is not included within the controlled vocabulary, then, except by accident, books will not be indexed with that term.

To illustrate the use of *Library of Congress Subject Headings*, we begin with the search term *intelligence*. Figure 3—E presents the entry for *Intelligence* (**23**) as it appears in the subject-headings list. The word is in light print with a *See* reference (**24**) indicating that this term is not used to index books; instead the entry refers us to the preferred term *Intellect*. Intellect (**25**) is printed in boldface, indicating that it is a main heading. Main headings are used as subject headings to index books in the card catalog. Following the main heading are several types of cross references and subdivisions. The *sa* (**26**), known as a *see also* reference, lists a number of related and more specific terms that can be consulted. Of particular interest is the narrower term *intelligence tests* (**27**), one of our original search terms. If we check the main entry under intelligence tests (**28**), we find that this term too appears in boldface as a main heading and has a number of more specific *see also* reference terms. In this case, the specific reference terms are particular tests, for example, *Binet-Simon test* and *Wechsler intelligence scale for children* (**29**). The suggested LC number for books about intelligence tests in general is BF431.5 (**30**). If your library has an open-stack system, you might browse the shelves around BF431.5 to identify other relevant materials.

Following the main heading for intellect in Figure 3—E, is an *x* (**31**), known as a *see from* reference, which indicates that the terms *Human intelligence, Intelligence,* and *Mind* are not used as subject headings. If you had looked up those terms, you would have been referred from those terms to the preferred term *Intellect*. This cross reference is consistent with the *see* reference (**24**) discussed above. The next item of possible interest is the *xx* (**32**), *see also from* reference, which means that terms such as *Ability* are broader and more general than *Intellect*. There will be a *see also* reference from those more general terms to the more specific term *Intellect*.

The list ends with subdivisions, specific narrow aspects of the

FIGURE 3—E

Entries from *Library of Congress Subject Headings* (1980), illustrating the identification of terms used as acceptable subject headings in the card catalog.

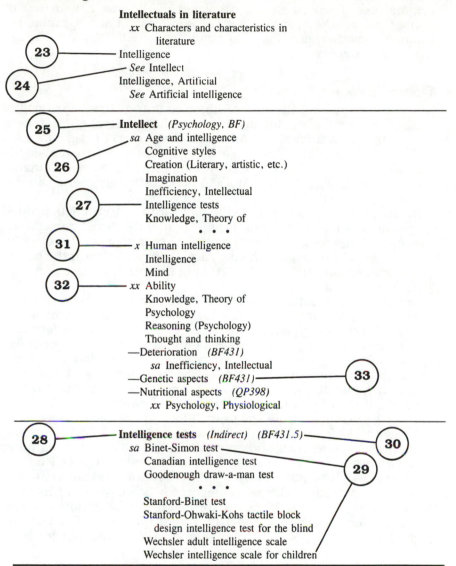

Intellectuals in literature
xx Characters and characteristics in
literature

23 —— Intelligence
See Intellect

24 —— Intelligence, Artificial
See Artificial intelligence

25 —— **Intellect** *(Psychology, BF)*
sa Age and intelligence
Cognitive styles

26 —— Creation (Literary, artistic, etc.)
Imagination
Inefficiency, Intellectual

27 —— Intelligence tests
Knowledge, Theory of
• • •

31 —— *x* Human intelligence
Intelligence
Mind

32 —— *xx* Ability
Knowledge, Theory of
Psychology
Reasoning (Psychology)
Thought and thinking
—Deterioration *(BF431)*
sa Inefficiency, Intellectual
—Genetic aspects *(BF431)* —— **33**
—Nutritional aspects *(QP398)*
xx Psychology, Physiological

28 —— **Intelligence tests** *(Indirect)* *(BF431.5)* —— **30**
sa Binet-Simon test
Canadian intelligence test
Goodenough draw-a-man test **29**
• • •
Stanford-Binet test
Stanford-Ohwaki-Kohs tactile block
design intelligence test for the blind
Wechsler adult intelligence scale
Wechsler intelligence scale for children

main heading. Of particular interest to us, in view of our topic, is the subdivision "—Genetic aspects" (**33**). Books that deal specifically with hereditary determinants of intelligence would be listed in the card catalog under the subject heading, INTELLECT—GENETIC ASPECTS. Cards for books of this type are usually filed alphabetically by author, after all entries under the more general heading INTELLECT. (For further information, consult the introduction in the subject-headings list.)

To summarize, we have identified the following legitimate subject headings: INTELLECT, INTELLECT—GENETIC ASPECTS, INTELLIGENCE TESTS,

NATURE AND NURTURE, and the names of a number of specific tests. We eliminated the following terms because they are not used as subject headings: intelligence, human intelligence, and mind. As we conducted the search, we would continue the process of revising the original list of search terms. We would modify the list further by using the tracings on the catalog cards of relevant monographs. For example, another heading that would eventually appear through this process is PSYCHOLOGICAL TESTS FOR MINORITIES.

Other Types of Catalogs

A small but growing number of libraries do not have a catalog of cards. The alternatives include book catalogs, microfiche catalogs, and computerized catalogs. Although these reproduction formats differ from a catalog of index cards, the content of the catalog is typically the same. Each type of catalog provides access to monographs by author, title, and subject and follows the general cataloging rules outlined above.

In the book catalog, the index to a library's collections is printed on paper and bound in book form. Frequently there are separate catalog volumes for each type of entry—author, title, and subject. In some cases, to save space, tracings are not provided with the bibliographic information for books, making essential the use of a subject-headings list.

Another type of catalog, especially in large libraries with multiple branches, is the microfiche catalog. Microfiche is a transparent plastic film record, typically 4″ x 6″ in size. Each sheet of microfiche may contain as many as 100 pages of information about thousands of books. A mechanical microfiche reader is needed to enlarge and illuminate the microfiche. With such a system having a complete list of the entire holdings of the library system in each branch library is possible. If the library has numerous branches, the microfiche record will probably indicate the branch location of each book.

A wave of the future is the on-line, randomly accessible, computerized catalog. Using a cathode ray tube (CRT) linked to a computer that contains the bibliographic records of the library's collections, one may search by author, title, subject, editor, and so forth.

We have presented the most important basic steps in locating monographs. You should now have enough information to begin searching for books and to do a good job with your search. If you find something that you do not understand, ask a librarian for help.

References

Bodmer, W. F., & Cavalli-Sforza, L. L. (1970). Intelligence and race. *Scientific American, 223*(4), 19–29.

Brazziel, W. F. (1969, December). *Perspectives on the Jensen Affair* (SuDoc HE 21.202: Im 7/7-1). Paper presented at the Head Start National Conference, Washington, DC.

Cronbach, L. J. (1975). Five decades of public controversy over mental testing. *American Psychologist, 30*, 1–14.

Haney, W. (1981). Validity, vaudeville, and values: A short history of social concerns over standardized testing. *American Psychologist, 36*, 1021–1034.

Herrnstein, R. J. (1971, September). I.Q. *Atlantic Monthly*, pp. 43–64.

Herrnstein, R. J. (1982, August). IQ testing and the media. *Atlantic Monthly*, pp. 68–74.

Jensen, A. R. (1969). How much can we boost IQ and scholastic achievement? *Harvard Educational Review, 39*, 1–123.

Jensen, A. R. (1972). *Genetics and education*. New York: Harper & Row.

Kamin, L. J. (1974). *The science and politics of I.Q.* Potomac, MD: Erlbaum.

McCall, R. B. (1970). Intelligence quotient pattern over age: Comparisons among siblings and parent-child pairs. *Science, 170*, 644–648.

Nixon, R. M. (1971). Special message to the Congress on education reform, March 3, 1970. In *Public Papers of the Presidents of the United States: Richard Nixon, containing the public messages, speeches and statements of the President, 1970* (SuDoc GS 4.113:970) (p. 231). Washington, DC: U.S. Government Printing Office.

Rowan, C. T. (1970, May). How racists use "science" to degrade black people. *Ebony*, pp. 31–40.

Spicker, H. H. (1969, November). *The influence of selected variables on the effectiveness of preschool programs for disadvantaged children* (SuDoc HE21.202:Im 7/2). A paper presented at the Head Start Conference, Los Angeles, CA.

U.S. Department of Health & Human Services, Office of Human Development Services, Head Start Bureau. (1980). *Head Start in the 1980's: Review and recommendations, a report requested by the President of the United States* (SuDoc HE23.1102:H34/3/980). Washington, DC: U. S. Department of Health & Human Services.

U.S. Senate. (1972). Discussion between E. Van Den Haag and Senator W. Mondale. In *Headstart, Child Development Legislation, 1972: Joint Hearings*, March 27, 1972, before the Subcommittee on Children and Youth and the Subcommittee on Employment, Manpower and Poverty, of the Committee on Labor and Public Welfare (SuDoc Y4.L11/2:H34/24/972) (pp. 19–21). Washington, DC: U. S. Government Printing Office.

4 *Psychological Abstracts*

Sources Discussed

Thesaurus of psychological index terms (3rd ed.). (1982). Washington, DC: American Psychological Association.

Psychological abstracts. (1927–present). Washington, DC: American Psychological Association. Monthly.

Cumulated subject index to Psychological Abstracts, 1927–1960 (2 vols.). (1966). Boston: G. K. Hall.

> *First supplement, 1961–1965*. (1968); *Second supplement, 1966–1968* (2 vols., 1971).

Cumulative subject index to Psychological Abstracts, 1969–1971 (2 vols.). (1972). Washington, DC: American Psychological Association.

> *1972–1974* (2 vols., 1975); *1975–1977* (2 vols., 1978); *1978–1980* (2 vols., 1981).

Author index to Psychological Index 1894 to 1935 and Psychological Abstracts 1927 to 1958 (5 vols.). (1960). Boston: G. K. Hall.

> *First supplement, 1959–1963* (1965); *Second supplement, 1964–1968* (2 vols., 1970).

Cumulative author index to Psychological Abstracts, 1969–1971. (1972). Washington, DC: American Psychological Association.

> *1972–1974* (1975); *1975–1977* (1978); *1978–1980* (1981).

JSAS: Catalog of selected documents in psychology. (1971–present). Washington, DC: American Psychological Association. Quarterly until 1983; since then entitled *Psychological Documents* and published semiannually.

Psychological index. (1894–1935). Washington, DC: American Psychological Association.

Most published psychological research appears in the form of journal articles. The card catalog, however, does not index specific articles within journals. *Psychological Abstracts* (*PA*) does provide indexing for journal articles; it is the most important single index to research in psychology.

PA is published monthly, and it includes monthly as well as cumulated author and subject indexes. For each article indexed, you will find complete bibliographic information and a brief nonevaluative summary of the article.

Chapter Example: Learned Helplessness

This chapter illustrates the use of *PA* by focusing on the topic of learned helplessness. In his introductory textbook, *Psychology*, Henry Gleitman defines learned helplessness as "a condition created by exposure to inescapable aversive events. This retards or prevents learning in subsequent situations in which escape or avoidance is possible" (Gleitman, 1981, p. A35). This phenomenon was initially demonstrated with dogs subjected to electrical shock that was inescapable. When later placed in a situation in which they could avoid the shocks, the dogs failed to do so. They had learned to be helpless. This research has been extended to human behavior in an attempt to explain certain kinds of depression (Gleitman, 1981, p. 148).

Gleitman refers to several major sources on learned helplessness written by Seligman (1975), Seligman, Klein, and Miller (1976), and Seligman and Maier (1967). After consulting these three references, we could begin a search by looking for other articles on this topic by these authors (an author search) and also by consulting the references listed in these articles for articles by other authors. However, because students most often begin using *PA* with a subject search, we will first illustrate a subject search. On the basis of preliminary reading, we might find the following subject-search terms to be useful: *learned helplessness, helplessness, escape learning, shock, inescapable electric shock,* and *avoidance learning*.

Thesaurus of Psychological Index Terms: The Subject Approach

The first step in a subject search using *PA* is to consult the *Thesaurus of Psychological Index Terms*. Published in 1982, the most recent edition of the *Thesaurus* is the key to the **controlled vocabulary** (words and phrases that have specific meanings and that are authorized for use in subject indexing) of *PA* subject indexes. If a subject-search term you are using is not included in the controlled vocabulary, then that term will not be used to index materials in *PA*, and you will not find any citations, even though relevant research may have been published. Therefore you must ascertain which of your subject-search terms will be useful.

The *Thesaurus* contains two major parts—the Relationship Section and the Rotated Alphabetical Terms Section. Begin by examining the Relationship Section, where terms are listed alphabetically. Figure 4–A presents an excerpt from the *Thesaurus* containing the term "Learned Helplessness" in boldface print (**1**). Underneath the term, the **scope note (SN)** provides an exact definition of the term as it will be used in the controlled vocabulary for *PA* subject indexing (**2**). Cross-references help you select subject terms by referring you from unacceptable terms to acceptable terms. Had we checked under the term *helplessness* we would have found an entry for "Helplessness (Learned)" with the note "**Use** Learned Helplessness" (**3**). This cross-reference leads from the unused term to one that is used and is consistent with the initial "Learned Helplessness" entry (**1**), which contains the note "**UF** [i.e., used for] Helplessness (Learned)" (**3a**). Other concepts and terms that are related (**R**) to the topic of learned helplessness are "Attribution," "Emotional States," and "Experimental Neuroses" (**4**). Under some subject terms are also

FIGURE 4—A

Thesaurus of Psychological Index Terms (3rd ed., 1982, pp. 77, 94), Relationship Section, illustrating subject-indexing terms contained in the controlled vocabulary and showing notes and cross-references.

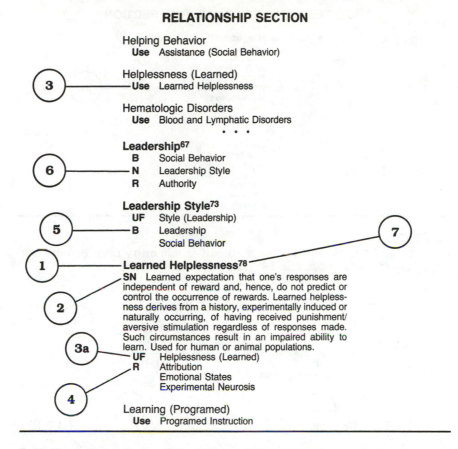

RELATIONSHIP SECTION

Helping Behavior
    Use Assistance (Social Behavior)

Helplessness (Learned)
    Use Learned Helplessness

Hematologic Disorders
    Use Blood and Lymphatic Disorders

• • •

Leadership[67]
    B   Social Behavior
    N   Leadership Style
    R   Authority

Leadership Style[73]
    UF Style (Leadership)
    B   Leadership
           Social Behavior

Learned Helplessness[78]
    SN Learned expectation that one's responses are independent of reward and, hence, do not predict or control the occurrence of rewards. Learned helplessness derives from a history, experimentally induced or naturally occurring, of having received punishment/aversive stimulation regardless of responses made. Such circumstances result in an impaired ability to learn. Used for human or animal populations.
    UF Helplessness (Learned)
    R   Attribution
           Emotional States
           Experimental Neurosis

Learning (Programed)
    Use Programed Instruction

listed broader, more general terms (**B**)(**5**) or narrower, more specific terms (**N**)(**6**) that are related to the term, although these do not appear under "Learned Helplessness." The number *78* (**7**) following "Learned Helplessness" indicates that the term was added to the controlled vocabulary in 1978. Thus, when you search subject indexes published before 1978, you must use search terms other than *learned helplessness.*

The second part of the *Thesaurus*, the Rotated Alphabetical Terms Section, is especially useful for identifying the correct entry for concepts expressed by several words or a phrase. In this section, illustrated in Figure 4—B, each term in a multiple-word indexing phrase appears in its proper alphabetical order. Entries in the subject indexes, however, are alphabetically arranged only by the first word in each indexing phrase. Thus, when we check either *helplessness* (**1a**) or *learned* (**1b**) in the rotated terms section, we find that the proper indexing term is *learned helplessness.* On the basis of this information, we can begin a subject search in a monthly issue of *PA*, looking for information indexed under the subject term *learned helplessness.*

FIGURE 4—B

Entries from the *Thesaurus of Psychological Index Terms* (3rd ed., 1982, pp. 212, 216), Rotated Alphabetical Terms Section, showing the correct entry form for multiple-word terms.

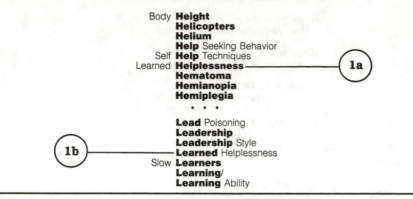

ROTATED ALPHABETICAL TERMS SECTION

Body **Height**
Helicopters
Helium
Help Seeking Behavior
Self **Help** Techniques
Learned **Helplessness** —————— 1a
Hematoma
Hemianopia
Hemiplegia
• • •

Lead Poisoning
Leadership
Leadership Style
1b ————— **Learned** Helplessness
Slow **Learners**
Learning/
Learning Ability

FIGURE 4—C

Subject- and author-index listings and an article entry from *Psychological Abstracts* (Vol. 65, June 1981, pp. xvi, xxxiv, 1225).

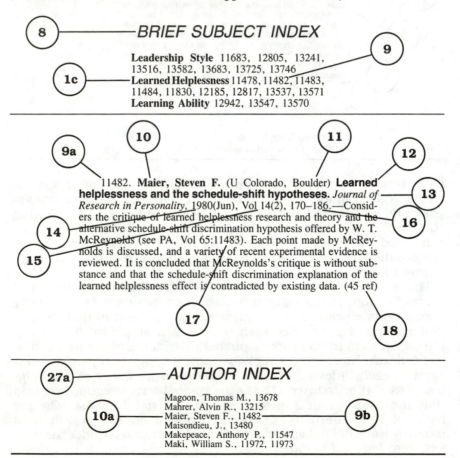

8 ————— *BRIEF SUBJECT INDEX*

Leadership Style 11683, 12805, 13241, 13516, 13582, 13683, 13725, 13746
1c — **Learned Helplessness** 11478, 11482, 11483, 11484, 11830, 12185, 12817, 13537, 13571
Learning Ability 12942, 13547, 13570

11482. **Maier, Steven F.** (U Colorado, Boulder) **Learned helplessness and the schedule-shift hypotheses.** *Journal of Research in Personality,* 1980(Jun), Vol 14(2), 170–186. —Considers the critique of learned helplessness research and theory and the alternative schedule-shift discrimination hypothesis offered by W. T. McReynolds (see PA, Vol 65:11483). Each point made by McReynolds is discussed, and a variety of recent experimental evidence is reviewed. It is concluded that McReynolds's critique is without substance and that the schedule-shift discrimination explanation of the learned helplessness effect is contradicted by existing data. (45 ref)

27a ————— *AUTHOR INDEX*

Magoon, Thomas M., 13678
Mahrer, Alvin R., 13215
Maier, Steven F., 11482 ————— 9b
Maisondieu, J., 13480
Makepeace, Anthony P., 11547
Maki, William S., 11972, 11973

Using *Psychological Abstracts*

The table of contents of the June, 1981, issue of *PA* indicates that articles in *PA* are arranged under broad subject categories, for example, "Physical and Psychological Disorders." This particular category is further divided into narrower subcategories, for example, "Mental Disorders" and "Speech and Language Disorders." To find citations on a more specific concept, however, we will have to consult the Brief Subject Index, located in the back of the monthly issue.

As shown in Figure 4–C, the term *learned helplessness* (**1c**) is listed in the Brief Subject Index (**8**). Following the term are nine numbers, known as entry numbers, corresponding to sources indexed in this issue of *PA*. To illustrate how to use this index, we start by finding entry number 11482 (**9**), although in an actual search we would eventually check all nine entry numbers. In each issue of *PA*, citations are listed consecutively by the entry number, which appears at the beginning of the citation. Each entry consists of two major parts: the bibliographic information, which will enable us to locate the publication, and a nonevaluative abstract summarizing the article.

Following the entry number (**9a**) in Figure 4–C is the author's name (**10**), arranged with last name first, and, in parentheses, the author's affiliation at the time the article was written and submitted for publication (**11**). In this example the author, Steven F. Maier, was affiliated with the University of Colorado at Boulder. The title of the article, here "Learned Helplessness and the Schedule-Shift Hypothesis" (**12**), appears next followed by information about the article's publication. Maier's article was published in the *Journal of Research in Personality* (**13**), in June 1980 (**14**), in Volume 14, issue number 2 (**15**), on pages 170 through 186 (**16**). Each entry for a journal article in *PA* employs this bibliographic format.

Following the citation is a brief abstract of the article. According to the abstract in Figure 4–C, Maier is responding to an article by W. T. McReynolds that is referenced in *PA*, Volume 65, entry 11483 (**17**). Thus the abstract of one article may lead you to the abstracts of other pertinent articles. Also, the abstract indicates whether the article itself has any information about further sources. In his article, Maier includes references to 45 other sources (**18**).

Volume Indexes to *Psychological Abstracts*

When a volume of *PA* is completed (when all 12 or, more recently, all 6 issues have been published), cumulated volume-indexes are compiled. A check of the term *learned helplessness* (**1d**) in the cumulated, semi-annual subject index to Volume 64 (1980, July–December) is illustrated in Figure 4–D. Note that the volume-cumulated Subject Index provides more information about each entry than the monthly Brief Subject Index. The second listing under the subject learned helplessness is of an entry that deals with "anxiety & associated cognitive interference," "performance decrement," and "college students" (**19**). This entry, which has the number 4732 (**20**), appears to be relevant to our search.

Entries are numbered sequentially throughout the issues of each volume, beginning with entry 1 in issue 1 of each volume. As illustrated in Figure 4–D, entry 4732 (**20a**) is listed under the general

FIGURE 4–D
Semiannual author- and subject-index listings and an article entry from *Psychological Abstracts* (Vol. 64, July–December 1980, pp. 12, 511, 596).

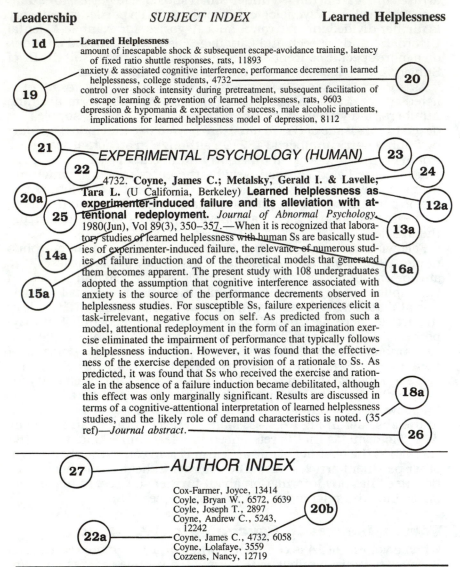

Leadership   *SUBJECT INDEX*   **Learned Helplessness**

Learned Helplessness
amount of inescapable shock & subsequent escape-avoidance training, latency of fixed ratio shuttle responses, rats, 11893
anxiety & associated cognitive interference, performance decrement in learned helplessness, college students, 4732
control over shock intensity during pretreatment, subsequent facilitation of escape learning & prevention of learned helplessness, rats, 9603
depression & hypomania & expectation of success, male alcoholic inpatients, implications for learned helplessness model of depression, 8112

EXPERIMENTAL PSYCHOLOGY (HUMAN)

4732. **Coyne, James C.; Metalsky, Gerald I. & Lavelle, Tara L.** (U California, Berkeley) **Learned helplessness as experimenter-induced failure and its alleviation with attentional redeployment.** *Journal of Abnormal Psychology,* 1980(Jun), Vol 89(3), 350–357.—When it is recognized that laboratory studies of learned helplessness with human Ss are basically studies of experimenter-induced failure, the relevance of numerous studies of failure induction and of the theoretical models that generated them becomes apparent. The present study with 108 undergraduates adopted the assumption that cognitive interference associated with anxiety is the source of the performance decrements observed in helplessness studies. For susceptible Ss, failure experiences elicit a task-irrelevant, negative focus on self. As predicted from such a model, attentional redeployment in the form of an imagination exercise eliminated the impairment of performance that typically follows a helplessness induction. However, it was found that the effectiveness of the exercise depended on provision of a rationale to Ss. As predicted, it was found that Ss who received the exercise and rationale in the absence of a failure induction became debilitated, although this effect was only marginally significant. Results are discussed in terms of a cognitive-attentional interpretation of learned helplessness studies, and the likely role of demand characteristics is noted. (35 ref)—*Journal abstract.*

AUTHOR INDEX

Cox-Farmer, Joyce, 13414
Coyle, Bryan W., 6572, 6639
Coyle, Joseph T., 2897
Coyne, Andrew C., 5243, 12242
Coyne, James C., 4732, 6058
Coyne, Lolafaye, 3559
Cozzens, Nancy, 12719

subject category of "Experimental Psychology (Human)" (**21**). The article represented by this entry has three authors: James C. Coyne (**22**), Gerald I. Metalsky (**23**), and Tara L. Lavelle (**24**), whose institutional affiliation is the University of California at Berkeley (**25**). As in the preceding example, the citation continues with the title of the article (**12a**), the name of the journal in which the article appears (**13a**), the year and month of publication (**14a**), the volume and issue numbers (**15a**), and the page numbers (**16a**). Following this information is the abstract. In this case the abstract is reprinted from the journal in which the full text of the article was published (**26**). The article contains 35 references (**18a**).

Author Indexes to *Psychological Abstracts*

If we had known that James C. Coyne had written on learned help-lessness, we could have used the Author Index to Volume 64. In the Author Index, the author and coauthor of each article included in the volume are listed in alphabetical order by surname. The Author Index (**27**) to Volume 64 is illustrated in Figure 4–D, showing the listing for James C. Coyne (**22a**), with citations for two entries. Entry 4732 (**20b**) is the same citation found earlier by using the Subject Index.

Similarly, as illustrated in Figure 4–C, we could have used the Author Index (**27a**) for recent issues of *PA* to locate articles by Steven F. Maier (**10a**). Such a search would have yielded entry 11482 (**9b**), the same article we identified when we used the Brief Subject Index.

At the beginning of the chapter, we mentioned several important early sources in the area of learned helplessness. One of those sources was written by Seligman and Maier and was published in 1967. As shown in Figure 4–E, the *PA* Author Index for Volume 41, covering the year 1967, identifies two entries for M. E. Seligman (**28**). Entry 8624 (**29**), found under the general subject heading "Animal Psychology" (**30**), turns out to be the article by Seligman (**28a**) and Maier (**10b**). This entry contains the standard information on institutional affiliation (**11b**), article title (**12b**), journal name (**13b**), year (**14b**), volume (**15b**), and pages (**16b**) and includes an abstract provided from the journal (**26b**).

Although we located this article published in 1967 in the *PA* volume issued in 1967, the search will not always be this easy. Sometimes, because of backlogs in processing or other problems, articles may be listed in a *PA* issue many months after the article's original publication. Therefore, you may have to consult several volumes of *PA* to find the information you need.

Extending the List of Search Terms

If we had attempted to search Volume 41 or any other pre-1978 Subject Index using the term *learned helplessness*, we would have found nothing because this indexing term was introduced into the *PA* controlled vocabulary in 1978. How could we search for our topic in pre-1978 *PA*? We would have to consult other, less specific terms included in the pre-1978 controlled vocabulary. Unfortunately, we could expect that, although useful, they would produce many irrelevant entries. What could we use as these subject-search terms? Recall that the original experiments mentioned in the textbook involved dogs subjected to shock in an escape/avoidance learning situation. Also, at the beginning of the search, we devised a list of possible search terms including *shock, inescapable electric shock, escape learning,* or *avoidance learning,* which might be useful here.

When we look for these terms, we find that the Subject Index (**8a**) to *PA*, Volume 41 (see Figure 4–E) uses two potentially relevant subject headings: "Escape" (**31**) and "Shock and Shock Intensity" (**32**). Next, we must examine numerous entries listed under each term to see if any are relevant. Scanning the list, we see that one entry under "Escape" deals with "avoidance learning, inescapable shock & subsequent interference," with research methods involving the use of a

FIGURE 4—E

Author- and subject-index listings for an early article on learned help-lessness by M. E. Seligman and S. F. Maier (article entry number 41:8624) from *Psychological Abstracts* (Vol. 41, January–December 1967, pp. 865, 1798, 2014, 2318).

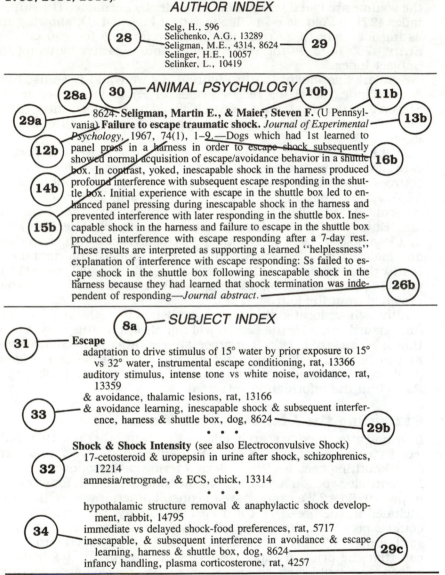

AUTHOR INDEX

(28)
Selg, H., 596
Selichenko, A.G., 13289
Seligman, M.E., 4314, 8624 (29)
Selinger, H.E., 10057
Selinker, L., 10419

ANIMAL PSYCHOLOGY

(28a) (30) (10b) (11b)

(29a) 8624. **Seligman, Martin E., & Maier, Steven F.** (U Pennsylvania) **Failure to escape traumatic shock.** *Journal of Experimental* (13b)
Psychology, 1967, 74(1), 1–9.—Dogs which had 1st learned to
(12b) panel press in a harness in order to escape shock subsequently
showed normal acquisition of escape/avoidance behavior in a shuttle (16b)
box. In contrast, yoked, inescapable shock in the harness produced
profound interference with subsequent escape responding in the shut-
(14b) tle box. Initial experience with escape in the shuttle box led to en-
hanced panel pressing during inescapable shock in the harness and
prevented interference with later responding in the shuttle box. Ines-
(15b) capable shock in the harness and failure to escape in the shuttle box
produced interference with escape responding after a 7-day rest.
These results are interpreted as supporting a learned "helplessness"
explanation of interference with escape responding: Ss failed to escape shock in the shuttle box following inescapable shock in the
harness because they had learned that shock termination was inde- (26b)
pendent of responding—*Journal abstract.*

SUBJECT INDEX

(8a)

(31) **Escape**
adaptation to drive stimulus of 15° water by prior exposure to 15°
vs 32° water, instrumental escape conditioning, rat, 13366
auditory stimulus, intense tone vs white noise, avoidance, rat,
13359
& avoidance, thalamic lesions, rat, 13166
(33) & avoidance learning, inescapable shock & subsequent interference, harness & shuttle box, dog, 8624 (29b)
• • •
Shock & Shock Intensity (see also Electroconvulsive Shock)
17-cetosteroid & uropepsin in urine after shock, schizophrenics,
(32) 12214
amnesia/retrograde, & ECS, chick, 13314
• • •
hypothalamic structure removal & anaphylactic shock development, rabbit, 14795
(34) immediate vs delayed shock-food preferences, rat, 5717
inescapable, & subsequent interference in avoidance & escape
learning, harness & shuttle box, dog, 8624 (29c)
infancy handling, plasma corticosterone, rat, 4257

"harness and shuttle box," and with a subject population "dog" (**33**). This reference carries the entry number 8624 (**29b**). A quick check shows this entry to be the Seligman and Maier article previously identified. The Subject Index term "Shock and Shock Intensity" lists one entry that deals with "inescapable" shock and its "subsequent interference in avoidance & escape learning" (**34**). This entry is also number 8624 (**29c**), the Seligman and Maier article. We now know that, although many irrelevant citations are included under these two terms, we can use the terms to continue searching successfully in other pre-1978 *PA* subject indexes.

Cumulated Indexes to *Psychological Abstracts*

By now you have probably gathered that this process is going to be laborious and time-consuming, and you may wonder whether any shortcuts exist. At the beginning of the chapter, we listed a number of cumulated or cumulative indexes. The cumulated subject and author indexes can be very useful. Instead of checking numerous volume indexes, you can check the less numerous cumulated indexes. The cumulated subject indexes have the same organization as the volume indexes and use the same subject headings; however, each entry includes the *PA* volume and entry number. Thus, had we checked the *Cumulated Subject Index to Psychological Abstracts, Second Supplement 1966–1968*, we would have found listed under the subject heading "Escape" the same entry by Seligman and Maier that was noted in Figure 4–E. Here the entry would be listed as 41:8624, indicating that the information is contained in *PA*, Volume 41 and has the entry number 8624.

The cumulated author indexes provide more complete information on citations than the monthly or volume indexes provide. Consequently, they are easier to use. Figure 4–F presents several sample entries for Martin E. Seligman as they appear in the 1969–1971 cumulation. Seligman has written several relevant articles on learned helplessness indexed during this three-year period—articles in the *Journal of Comparative and Physiological Psychology*, in *Psychonomic Science*, and in *Psychology Today*.

In many cases a publication is written by two or more coauthors. For example, the third reference in Figure 4–F was written by Martin E. Seligman and Dennis P. Groves. It is possible that the second author, Dennis P. Groves, has also written other relevant articles and that he is the first author on some of those articles. We can thus

FIGURE 4–F
Entries for M. E. Seligman from the *Cumulated Author Index to Psychological Abstracts, 1969–1971 (p. 545).*

Psychological Abstracts 1969–1971

Seligman, Martin E. Chronic fear produced by unpredictable electric shock. *Journal of Comparative & Physiological Psychology 1968, 66(2), 402–411.*   Vol.43:554

Seligman, Martin E.; *Ives, Charles E.; Ames, Harold; Mineka, Susan.* Conditioned drinking and its failure to extinguish: Avoidance, preparedness, or functional autonomy? *Journal of Comparative & Physiological Psychology 1970, 71(3), 411–419.*   Vol.44:12129

Seligman, Martin E.; *Groves, Dennis P.* Nontransient learned helplessness. *Psychonomic Science 1970, 19(3), 191–192.*
                    Vol.44:16234

Seligman, Martin E.; *Bravman, Susan; Radford, Robert.* Drinking: Discriminative conditioning in the rat. *Psychonomic Science 1970, 20(1), 63–64.*   Vol.44:20483

Seligman, Martin E. For helplessness: Can we immunize the weak? *Psychology Today 1969, Jun, Vol. 3(1), 42–44.*
                    Vol.46:734

Seligman, Martin E. On the generality of the laws of learning. *Psychological Review 1970, Sep, Vol. 77(5), 406–418.*
                    Vol.45:1675

Seligman, Martin E.; *Meyer, Bruce.* Chronic fear and ulcers in rats as a function of the unpredictability of safety. *Journal of Comparative & Physiological Psychology 1970, Oct, Vol. 73(2), 202–207.*   Vol.45:5852

TABLE 4–A

**Topics Included in *Psychological Abstracts*
as Relevant or Related to Psychology, and Topics
Excluded From *PA* as Irrelevant***

Relevant	Related	Irrelevant
sexual behavior	sexual hormones	fertility patterns
smoking behavior	nicotine pharmacology	lung cancer
verbal com- munication	linguistics	vocal-cord physiology
man–machine systems	technology and work	computer programming

Note: *Psychological Abstracts Information Services: Users Reference Manual* (1981, p. 1–1) uses the terms "Psychology," "Fringe Areas," and "Nonrelevant," respectively.

expand our author search by including coauthors when checking *PA* indexes.

The cumulated index contains the complete bibliographic information for each entry. If you wish to check the abstract to determine whether the article is relevant, the index provides the *PA* volume and entry numbers. You will find this information important if your library does not own a particular journal and you must judge whether to request an article through interlibrary loan, especially if there is a monetary charge for interlibrary loan service (see chapter 11).

Subject Scope of *Psychological Abstracts*

Since it was initiated in 1927, *PA* has become the most comprehensive indexing tool available to access the published literature of psychology. Selected sources from related disciplines, such as biology, education, management, medicine, psychiatry, social work, and sociology, are also included in *PA*. Each month *PA* indexers scan numerous journals and documents in these related fields. When the indexers determine that a particular article or document relates to psychology, they include it in *PA*. Table 4–A includes examples of materials from three categories: relevant (Psychology), related (Fringe Areas), and irrelevant (Nonrelevant) to psychology (American Psychological Association, 1981).

Examining Table 4–A, we note that verbal communication is a topic that could logically be pursued in *PA* because it concerns human behavior and interactions. Depending upon what aspect of linguistics one needed to examine, *PA* might provide useful information on the topic. But vocal cord physiology, although related to verbal communication, would not be suitable for inclusion in *PA*. For this topic, you would need to consult a more appropriate indexing tool in medicine or speech pathology. (For more information about related sources, see chapter 5.)

Sources of Citations in *Psychological Abstracts*

Journal articles compose the majority of citations to the professional literature included in *PA*; however, literature in other formats has also been included. Doctoral dissertations, which are typically

FIGURE 4–G
Entries for doctoral dissertations on learned helplessness from *Psychological Abstracts* (Vol. 62, 1979, p. 1323).

EXPERIMENTAL PSYCHOLOGY (HUMAN)   62: 12906–12919

Motivation & Emotion

12907. **Abramson, Lyn Y.** (U Pennsylvania) **Universal versus personal helplessness: An experimental test of the reformulated theory of learned helplessness.** *Dissertation Abstracts International*, 1979(Jan), Vol 39(7-B), 3495–3496.   **35**

• • •

12909. **Bowles, Janet M.** (Michigan State U) **An investigation of affective facial expressions in a learned helplessness paradigm.** *Dissertation Abstracts International*, 1979(Jan), Vol 39(7-B), 3499–3500.

not published, are an important part of the original research literature of psychology. Until 1980 *PA* provided access to dissertations reported in the psychology section of *Dissertation Abstracts International (DAI)*. Figure 4–G shows typical citations for doctoral dissertations on learned helplessness. These entries are similar to journal-article entries, with two important differences: (1) Abstracts do not accompany entries for dissertations, and (2) you will always be referred to *DAI* (35) for further information, including a lengthy abstract. *DAI* will also provide information about ordering a doctoral dissertation should it be essential for your research. (See chapter 11 for further information on *DAI*.)

Books and chapters within books also compose a small but important part of the literature of psychology. Figure 4–H illustrates an entry from *PA*, Volume 54 (1975) that describes a book written by Martin E. Seligman (28b) and entitled *Helplessness: On Depression, Development, and Death* (36). Provided are the place of publication (37), the publisher (38), the date of publication (39), and descriptive information including an abstract (40). You may recall that this book is one of the references Gleitman (1981) provided.

Two types of book-chapter entries are illustrated in Figure 4–I. The first, entry 7618 from *PA*, Volume 53 (1975), is a chapter by Seligman in a book edited by R. J. Friedman and M. M. Katz (41), entitled *The Psychology of Depression: Contemporary Theory and*

FIGURE 4–H
A book entry from *Psychological Abstracts* (Vol. 54, 1975, p. 162).

54: 1313–1320   *PHYSICAL AND PSYCHOLOGICAL DISORDERS*

28b 1316. **Seligman, Martin E.** (U Pennsylvania) **Helplessness:**   **36**
On depression, development, and death. San Francisco, CA:
38 W. H. Freeman, 1975. xv, 250 p. $8.95.—Presents evidence contributing to the theory that anxiety and depression grow out of a   **37**
feeling of helplessness and that this feeling must be learned. It is
suggested that when depressed individuals are guided through situa-
39 tions in which they learn to exert greater control on their environ-   **40**
ments, their depression dissipates. The author's experimental work
with animals and case histories of persons suffering from anxiety and
depression are reviewed. (30 p ref)

FIGURE 4–I

Book-chapter entries in *Psychological Abstracts.* (The top reference is to a chapter in a collection edited by R. J. Friedman and M. M. Katz, indexed in *Psychological Abstracts* [Vol. 53, 1975, p. 943]. The bottom entry refers to a chapter in the *Annual Review,* indexed in *Psychological Abstracts* [Vol. 62, 1979, p. 1143].)

PHYSICAL AND PSYCHOLOGICAL DISORDERS 53: 7614–7621

7618. **Seligman, Martin E.** (U Pennsylvania) **Depression and learned helplessness.** In R. J. Friedman & M. M. Katz (Eds), *The psychology of depression: Contemporary theory and research.* New York, NY: John Wiley & Sons, 1974, xvii, 318 p. $15. **(41)**

EXPERIMENTAL SOCIAL PSYCHOLOGY 62: 10992–11003

10997. **DeCharms, Richard & Muir, Marion S.** (Washington U Graduate Inst of Education, MO) **Motivation: Social approaches.** *Annual Review of Psychology,* 1978, Vol 29, 91–113.— Presents a critique based on the thesis that present criteria for evaluation of research are laden with methodological dictates and lack maxims to promote theoretical and practical relevance. Recent work by J. W. Atkinson and work begun under his guidance, D. C. McClelland's recent work on the power motive, M. E. P. Seligman's "learned helplessness" and its relationship to J. W. Brehm's psychological reactance, work on personal causation, and current work on extrinsic rewards and intrinsic motivation are highlighted. (136 ref)

Research. The second, entry 10997 from *PA,* Volume 62 (1979), written by R. DeCharms and M. S. Muir, is a chapter in the 1978 *Annual Review of Psychology* **(42).**

In some cases, complete bibliographic information on a book chapter is not provided with the entry. In such a case, you must check the main entry for the book, listed under the name of the first editor. You can find the main entry by using the author index to the particular *PA* volume with which you are working.

Since 1980, citations to books, book chapters, and dissertations have not been included in the printed issues of *PA.* Entries for doctoral dissertations, however, are still included in the *PA* data base and may be retrieved by a computer search (for details, see chapter 8).

From time to time *PA* enters articles from foreign-language publications. In some cases, an entire article is published in a language other than English; in other cases, the journal will provide an English translation or summary. In the latter situation, information within the *PA* entry will indicate the language of the original article. It may also show whether a summary is available in English.

A relatively new source of information that *PA* includes is *Psychological Documents* (formerly called *Catalog of Selected Documents in Psychology*). This catalog provides information about manuscripts that are too long or otherwise unsuitable for journal publication and are not published as books. Figure 4–J, showing an entry in *PA,* presents information about an unpublished bibliography of research on learned helplessness listed in the *Catalog.* The 23-page bibliography is available in paper copy for $5.00 or in microfiche for $3.00.

Background on *Psychological Abstracts*

The coverage that *PA* provides of the professional literature of psychology is continually expanding. The 1969–1971 *Cumulative Subject Index* noted that, during that three-year period, over 800 journals and 1200 books, dissertations, and other materials were scanned for possible inclusion. In 1981, approximately 1000 journals were regularly scanned. The increase in coverage may be readily seen in Figure 4–K, which notes the number of entries appearing in one year of *PA* at ten-year intervals since 1930. Since 1960 publishing in psychology has had an especially rapid growth.

The researcher whose topic requires an historical overview of the research may be interested in the predecessor to *PA. Psychological Index,* originally published in connection with the scholarly journal *Psychological Review,* began in 1894 as an annual bibliography of psychology and related topics. It was a bibliographic supplement to

FIGURE 4–J

A listing for a bibliography on learned helplessness available through *Psychological Documents* (formerly called the *Catalog of Selected Documents in Psychology*). (This entry appeared in *Psychological Abstracts* [Vol. 64, 1980, p. 1002].)

9342. **Kirk, Raymond C. & Blampied, Neville M.** (U Canterbury, Christchurch, New Zealand) **A bibliography of learned helplessness research.** *Catalog of Selected Documents in Psychology,* 1980(Feb), Vol 10, 19–20. MS. 2029 (23 p/paper: $5; fiche: $3).

FIGURE 4–K

Number of entries included in *Psychological Abstracts* in 6 different years, showing the increase in coverage of *Psychological Abstracts* and reflecting an increase in publications. (Note: Unlike 1970, 1980 does not include dissertations or books.)

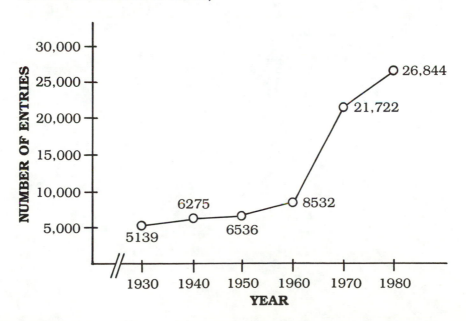

the *Review*, published by the American Psychological Association, and it continued to appear after *PA* was initiated in 1927. *Psychological Index* ceased publication after its 1935 volume was issued because of a decision by the APA that the two sources were duplicative. After 1935, access to psychological literature was provided by *PA*.

The chapters that follow describe sources which supplement *PA*. These may contain useful information particularly in areas of psychology that overlap with other fields such as education, management, medicine, and sociology. Additional specialized sources are included in Appendix A.

References

American Psychological Association. (1981). *PsycINFO Psychological Abstracts information services: Users reference manual.* Washington, DC: Author.

Gleitman, H. (1981). *Psychology.* New York: Norton.

Seligman, M. E. (1975). *Helplessness: On depression, development and death.* San Francisco: Freeman.

Seligman, M. E., Klein, D. C., & Miller, W. R. (1976). Depression. In H. Leitenberg (Ed.), *Handbook of behavior modification and behavior therapy* (pp. 168–210). Englewood Cliffs, NJ: Prentice-Hall.

Seligman, M. E., & Maier, S. F. (1967). Failure to escape traumatic shock. *Journal of Experimental Psychology, 74,* 1–9.

5 Psychology-Related Indexing and Abstracting Tools

Although *Psychological Abstracts (PA)* is the primary tool providing access to psychological literature, many indexing and abstracting services in related areas are of potential interest to psychologists. This chapter will present indexing and abstracting tools in several psychology-related disciplines. For example, educational literature may be of interest to the educational psychologist and management literature to the industrial/organizational or consumer psychologist. Abnormal and social psychologists may wish to examine literature in sociology, whereas physiological, clinical, and comparative psychologists will find literature in medicine and biology relevant. This chapter is divided into four sections, presenting sources which provide access to literature in education, management, sociology, and medicine. As in previous chapters, the discussions center on sample search topics relevant to the sources discussed. The selected sources supplement references found in *PA*.

1 Education

Sources Discussed

Resources in education. (1966–present). Washington, DC: U.S. Department of Education, National Institute of Education. Formerly *Research in Education.* Monthly.

> *Index.* (1967–1979). Washington, DC: U.S. Department of Health, Education, & Welfare, National Institute of Education. Annual, 1967–1974. Semiannual, 1975–1979.

> *Index.* (1980–present). Phoenix, AZ: Oryx Press. Annual.

Slawsky, D. A. (Ed.). (1980). *Directory of ERIC microfiche collections.* Washington, DC: Educational Resources Information Center.

Current index to journals in education. (1969–present). Phoenix, AZ: Oryx Press. Monthly, cumulated annually, 1969–1974, semiannually, 1975–present.

Thesaurus of ERIC descriptors (9th ed.). (1982). Phoenix, AZ: Oryx Press.

Education index. (1929–present). New York: H. W. Wilson. Monthly, cumulated annually.

Section Example: Effects of Teacher Expectations on Minority Student Success

In his textbook on educational psychology, R. F. Biehler (1978) describes research concerning teacher expectations of student performance. Especially interesting is his description of demonstrations by R. Rosenthal and L. Jacobson (1968) that a teacher's expectations of students influence how the students perform in a classroom setting. Biehler calls this influence the "Pygmalion effect"; others have used the terms "self-fulfilling prophecy" and "teacher expectation" (Biehler, 1978, p. 24). Limiting the topic, we concentrate in this section on the differential impact that teachers may have on minority children, more precisely the effects of classroom teacher expectations on minority student success, to illustrate a literature search with important education sources.

Educational Resources Information Center (ERIC)

The Educational Resources Information Center (ERIC) was established in 1966 as part of the U.S. Office of Education. The initial purpose of ERIC was to provide access to documents produced as a result of education-related government programs and grants, many of which were not widely published or distributed. "Including a network of information clearinghouses, [ERIC] acquires, abstracts, indexes, stores, retrieves, and disseminates educational research information" (U.S. Department of Health, Education, & Welfare, 1967, p. 184). Today 16 ERIC clearinghouses, each responsible for a particular subject area, cover a broad range of interests, many types of research, and many forms of research reporting whether or not sponsored by the government. Many psychologists are interested in ERIC's coverage of educational psychology, testing, counseling, child development, and evaluation research.

ERIC provides three important resources for the researcher. The first is *Resources in Education (RIE*, formerly, *Research in Education)*, published monthly with annual cumulated indexes. *RIE* indexes and includes abstracts of conference proceedings, position papers, research reports, curriculum guides, books, doctoral dissertations, and other types of materials collected and processed by ERIC clearinghouses.

The second service is document delivery. More than 700 libraries in the United States (primarily college and university libraries) subscribe to the ERIC Document Microfiche Collection, which makes available most documents indexed in *RIE*. On a monthly basis, subscribing libraries receive shipments of microfiche for documents included in recent issues of *RIE*. Subscribing libraries are listed in the *Directory of ERIC Microfiche Collections*. Copies of most ERIC documents, available in paper copy or microfiche, are also sold by the ERIC Document Reproduction Service at a reasonable cost.

The third ERIC service is *Current Index to Journals in Education (CIJE)*. First published in 1969, *CIJE* provides access to over 750 journals in education and related disciplines. Subject and author indexes in *CIJE* and *RIE* appear in each monthly issue and are cumulated.

Thesaurus of ERIC Descriptors

The source of controlled vocabulary for both *RIE* and *CIJE* is the *Thesaurus of ERIC Descriptors*. We begin our search by consulting this volume. Using the search terms we originally identified (Pygmalion effect, self-fulfilling prophecy, teacher expectations), we examine the section of the *Thesaurus* entitled the Alphabetical Descriptor Display, which is an alphabetical list of the controlled vocabulary in ERIC's publications. We discover, however, that the suggested search terms are not in the descriptor display and thus are not useful for searching *RIE* or *CIJE*. To proceed, we must be creative in finding search terms that can be used successfully. One approach is to identify synonyms of the terms with which we started. Another approach is to consult the section of the *Thesaurus* called the Rotated Descriptor Display (similar to the Rotated Alphabetical Terms section of the *Thesaurus of Psychological Index Terms*; see chapter 4). When we check the three original search terms there, we see that "Pygmalion effect" and "self-fulfilling prophesy" do not lead to relevant descriptors. "Teacher expectations" leads to many descriptors containing the word *teacher*, none of which appear relevant. As illustrated in Figure 5–A, however, *expectation* (1), another possibility, does appear in the Rotated Display of Descriptors. This term, rather than *expectancy*, is used by ERIC, as indicated by the "Use EXPECTATION" cross-reference (2).

Returning to the Alphabetical Descriptor Display in the *Thesaurus* for further information about the term *expectation* (1a), we learn that the term has been a part of the ERIC controlled vocabulary since 1969 (3). Since December, 1969, it has been used to index 843 documents in *CIJE* (4) and 660 documents in *RIE* (5). These numbers are potentially useful information: A frequently used descriptor may be too broad and may cover many irrelevant references, whereas an infrequently used descriptor may yield a small number of relevant

FIGURE 5—A

Entries from the *Thesaurus of ERIC Descriptors* (9th ed., pp. 87, 328), 1982.

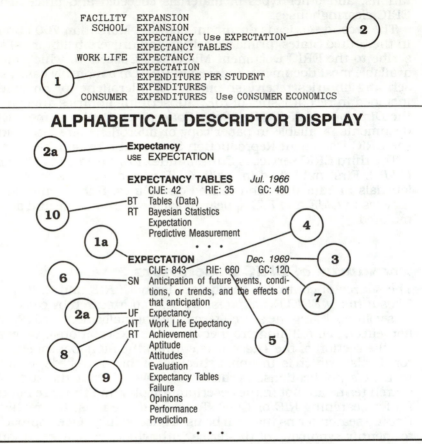

ROTATED DESCRIPTOR DISPLAY

```
    FACILITY  EXPANSION
      SCHOOL  EXPANSION
                EXPECTANCY   Use EXPECTATION
                EXPECTANCY TABLES
   WORK LIFE  EXPECTANCY
               EXPECTATION
                EXPENDITURE PER STUDENT
                EXPENDITURES
    CONSUMER  EXPENDITURES  Use CONSUMER ECONOMICS
```

ALPHABETICAL DESCRIPTOR DISPLAY

Expectancy
USE EXPECTATION

EXPECTANCY TABLES   *Jul. 1966*
    CIJE: 42   RIE: 35   GC: 480
BT Tables (Data)
RT Bayesian Statistics
    Expectation
    Predictive Measurement

• • •

EXPECTATION   *Dec. 1969*
    CIJE: 843   RIE: 660   GC: 120
SN Anticipation of future events, condi-
    tions, or trends, and the effects of
    that anticipation
UF Expectancy
NT Work Life Expectancy
RT Achievement
    Aptitude
    Attitudes
    Evaluation
    Expectancy Tables
    Failure
    Opinions
    Performance
    Prediction

• • •

references. The scope note (**SN**) (**6**) provides a brief explanation of the term's index usage. *Expectation* has broad applicability; thus few of the references will deal with expectations of teachers, and fewer will deal with minority students.

To supplement the terms listed below the descriptor, we could also consult the Descriptor Group Code (**GC**) section of the *Thesaurus* (**7**). GC codes represent broad concepts under which related descriptors are listed. We would use the GC primarily with a computer search to expand the list of search terms. For further information, consult the ERIC *Thesaurus*. The **UF** and **USE** (**2a**) cross references restate the inclusion of *expectation* instead of *expectancy*. Narrower, more specific terms are listed following **NT** (**8**), and related terms follow **RT** (**9**). Broader terms (**BT**), although not included under the heading "Expectation," are illustrated in the preceding entry (**10**.)

Having found relevant, acceptable indexing terms by using the *Thesaurus*, we can now use these terms for searching in *RIE* and *CIJE* subject indexes.

FIGURE 5–B

Subject Index entries from *Resources in Education Annual Cumulation: Index 1980* (p. 225), 1981.

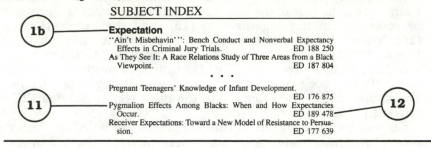

FIGURE 5–C

Portions of a document resume from *Resources in Education* (Vol. 15, p. 36), December 1980.

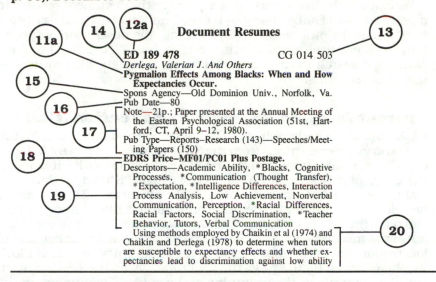

Resources in Education (RIE)

Presented in Figure 5–B is a portion of the *RIE* Subject Index (Vol. 15) showing several document title entries, listed in alphabetical order, that follow the heading "Expectation" (**1b**). Among these entries is "Pygmalion Effects Among Blacks . . . Occur" (**11**), which appears to be relevant to our search. This entry, like each ERIC document, is assigned a unique accession number, beginning with the letters **ED** (ERIC Document) and followed by a six digit number (**12**). The accession number refers us to the appropriate entry in the Document Resume section.

Document resumes, listed sequentially by ED number, provide bibliographic information and a lengthy abstract for each document that is entered. Figure 5–C presents the *RIE* document resume for a title that interests us, ED 189 478. The ERIC accession number (**12a**) is at the upper left-hand corner of the entry. An additional number (**13**), assigned by the ERIC clearinghouse that originally processed the document, appears at the upper right-hand corner. This is a temporary accession number given before an ED number has been assigned. Such clearinghouse numbers occasionally appear in a document abstract referring to related documents in a series. Bibliographic information, including the name(s) of the author(s) (**14**), the title of the publication (**11a**), the sponsoring agency or research-funding organization (**15**), and the publication date (**16**), follows. "Notes" and "Pub Type" (**17**) describe the source and type of document. "EDRS Price" (**21**) indicates that this item is available for purchase from the ERIC Document Reproduction Service. "MF01/PC01" are price codes needed for ordering this document. You should check the price list in the most recent issue of *RIE* for current prices.

Subject terms assigned to this document are listed as "Descriptors" (**19**). A maximum of six major descriptors, indicated by asterisks (*), may be assigned to a document and used as subject headings in print indexes. Finally, a lengthy abstract (**20**) summarizes the document's contents.

We can use the list of major descriptors in the document resume to modify our list of subject-search terms. This list of major descriptors is especially helpful because, if you recall, the descriptor "Expectation" was not used until December 1969 (see Figure 5–A) and expanding a search to cover material before this date will require the use of other terms.

Current Index to Journals in Education (CIJE)

CIJE, similar in approach to *RIE*, indexes journal literature. Figure 5–D shows several entries from the Subject Index of the 1977, January–June, semiannual cumulation of *CIJE*, which we located using the descriptor "Expectation" (**1c**). The article "Students' Race, Social Class, and Academic History . . . Performance" (**21**) appears to be relevant to our topic. Because only limited information is provided for the article in this index (**22**)—for example, the name of the author is missing—we must use the *CIJE* accession number (**23**) to locate more complete information in the Main Entry section of *CIJE*. As illustrated in Figure 5–E, the ERIC Journal (**EJ**) accession number (**23a**) appears at the beginning of the entry. The number on the right side is the ERIC clearinghouse accession number (**13a**). This number is followed by the title of the article (**21a**), the name of the author (**24**), and the full citation (**22a**). Also provided is a list of descriptors assigned to this article (**25**) and a brief summary of the article's contents (**26**).

Another Approach to RIE and CIJE

Suppose that you are able to begin a search with a relevant source. Rather than start with the *Thesaurus*, you could first locate the document in *RIE* or *CIJE* by using the author or institution indexes in *RIE* or the author or journal contents indexes in *CIJE*. (In some years an *RIE* title index will also be available.) Then you could screen the list of major descriptors assigned to your source in the Main Entry or Document Resume sections to create or modify a list of relevant subject-search terms. As a double check, you could consult the *Thesaurus* for other potentially relevant terms and proceed with the search.

FIGURE 5–D
Subject Index entries from the *Current Index to Journals in Education* (p. 737), January–June 1977.

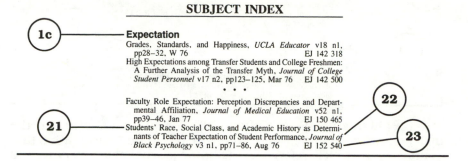

SUBJECT INDEX

1c — **Expectation**
Grades, Standards, and Happiness, *UCLA Educator* v18 n1, pp28–32, W 76   EJ 142 318
High Expectations among Transfer Students and College Freshmen: A Further Analysis of the Transfer Myth, *Journal of College Student Personnel* v17 n2, pp123–125, Mar 76   EJ 142 500
• • •
Faculty Role Expectation: Perception Discrepancies and Departmental Affiliation, *Journal of Medical Education* v52 n1, pp39–46, Jan 77   EJ 150 465 — **22**
21 — Students' Race, Social Class, and Academic History as Determinants of Teacher Expectation of Student Performance, *Journal of Black Psychology* v3 n1, pp71–86, Aug 76   EJ 152 540 — **23**

FIGURE 5–E
A citation from the Main Entry section of *Current Index to Journals in Education* (p. 534), January–June 1977.

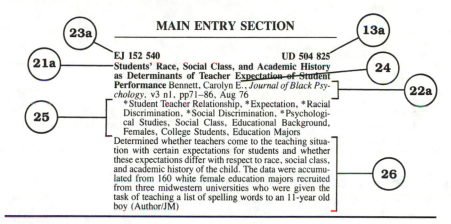

MAIN ENTRY SECTION   **13a**

23a — EJ 152 540   UD 504 825
21a — **Students' Race, Social Class, and Academic History as Determinants of Teacher Expectation of Student Performance** Bennett, Carolyn E., *Journal of Black Psychology*, v3 n1, pp71–86, Aug 76 — **24** / **22a**
25 — *Student Teacher Relationship, *Expectation, *Racial Discrimination, *Social Discrimination, *Psychological Studies, Social Class, Educational Background, Females, College Students, Education Majors
Determined whether teachers come to the teaching situation with certain expectations for students and whether these expectations differ with respect to race, social class, and academic history of the child. The data were accumulated from 160 white female education majors recruited from three midwestern universities who were given the task of teaching a list of spelling words to an 11-year old boy (Author/JM) — **26**

Education Index

Some libraries subscribe to *Education Index* (*EI*), published by H. W. Wilson, as an alternative to *CIJE*. Initiated in 1929, published monthly and cumulated annually, *EI* is useful for searching education journal literature published before 1969. Some students find *EI* easier to use than *CIJE*, possibly because of its similarity to the *Readers' Guide to Periodical Literature.* There is no thesaurus. Author and subject entries are included in the same alphabetical index with "see" cross references directing the user from unused terms to authorized subject headings. *EI* has its limitations, however. It covers only the core journals in education and special education (about 300 titles) and, therefore, has a much more limited scope than *CIJE*. Furthermore, it provides no abstracts.

Figure 5–F presents excerpts that follow the subject heading "Expectation (Psychology)" (**27**) in the December, 1981, issue of *EI*. Listed under boldface subject headings, citations are arranged alphabetically by title. A reference potentially relevant to our topic is "Effects of students' ethnicity and sex on the expectations of teach-

FIGURE 5–F
Entries from *Education Index*, December 1981, *53*(4), 119.

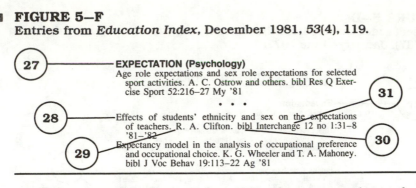

ers" (**28**), written by R. A. Clifton (**29**). The citation shows that the article contains a bibliography (**30**). The remaining information (**31**) completes the article reference, including journal name, volume and issue numbers, number of pages, and date of publication. In the front of each issue appears a list of abbreviations of publications indexed. Because journal titles are often abbreviated in *EI* citations, you should consult the list so that you will not try to locate a journal that does not exist.

2 Management

Sources Discussed
Business periodicals index. (1958–present). New York: H. W. Wilson. Monthly (except August), cumulated annually.
Business index. (1980–present). Menlo Park, CA: Information Access Corp. Monthly.

Section Example: Job-Related Stress
In discussing the psychological costs of work, W. W. Rambo (1982) raises the issue of role conflict and points to research by R. L. Kahn (1974). Individuals in a work situation typically face expectations from several individuals or groups. When managers are caught between the conflicting expectations of supervisors and subordinates, they experience role conflict. Interviewing numerous individuals, Kahn and his associates (1964) found that role conflict was associated with high levels of job-related stress. We begin searching in order to learn more about role conflict and job-related stress.

Business Periodicals Index
Business Periodicals Index (*BPI*) provides access to more than 250 publications of three types: trade and industry journals; research journals in business, management, accounting, finance, and related areas; and selected journals from related disciplines. Monthly and annually cumulated issues provide alphabetical indexing by subject and author. *BPI* is similar to *EI* and other indexes published by H. W. Wilson.

In Figure 5–G, the subject heading "Role conflict" (**32**) identifies several relevant citations listed in alphabetical order by title. One citation that deals with role conflict and role stress is "Person/role

FIGURE 5–G
Entries from *Business Periodicals Index: 1980–1981 Annual Cumulation* (Vol. 23, p. 1228), August 1980–July 1981.

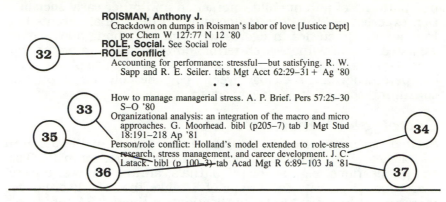

conflict . . . development" (**33**), written by J. C. Latack (**34**). The citation indicates that the article contains a bibliography (**35**) and tables (**36**). The entry also includes the abbreviated journal title, the volume number, the page numbers, and the publication date (**37**). You can decipher the abbreviations by consulting a list in the front of each issue and volume of *BPI*.

Business Index

Business Index, begun in 1980, covers more than 500 business periodicals. This indexing tool also includes references to articles in several influential daily and weekly newspapers, selective coverage of 1100 periodicals in related disciplines, and selected books and government publications. Entries are indexed by subject, author, and title with selected abstracting. Presently *Business Index* is available only on microfilm. Each month a subscribing library receives a new microfilm containing all indexing from the most recent three years. In late 1983, a bound volume is to be published containing all 1979 citations. Then, as current indexing is added and annual printed volumes are produced, the oldest references will be deleted from microfilm. Because this source is new, its format and publication schedule are subject to change.

3 Sociology

Source Discussed

Sociological abstracts. (1953–present). San Diego, CA: Sociological Abstracts. Five issues per year, annually cumulated indexes.

Section Example: Role of Parent-Child Interaction in Adolescent Aggressive Behavior

J. W. McDavid and H. Harari (1974) describe asocial behavior as a "consequence of a breakdown in the socialization of the individual," resulting in frustration and aggressive behavior (p. 120). They report research conducted by A. Bandura and R. Walters (1963) that showed that excessive aggression resulted from "breakdowns of normal patterns of parent-child interaction and other early socialization experiences" (p. 120). By focusing on the role of parent-child interaction difficulties in aggressive behavior among adolescents, we listed the following search terms: *parent-child interaction, aggressive behavior,* and *adolescents.* Because the disciplines of social psychology and sociology overlap considerably, we might find consulting sources in sociology advantageous.

Sociological Abstracts (SA)

Sociological Abstracts (*SA*) is the primary index for literature in sociology and its related disciplines. It includes articles in 1200 serial publications (e.g., scholarly journals, annual reviews, and research paper series). Each issue of *SA*, like that of *PA*, organizes literature in broad subject classifications. Although *SA* contains a grouping for social psychology (including small groups, leadership, personality, and culture), our primary access to information is through the subject index provided in each issue and in each annual cumulated volume. *SA* does not publish a thesaurus. Instead, its subject indexes present a series of key terms as index entries. These key terms are not as precise as descriptors, but they are relatively consistent from volume to volume. An identifying phrase (similar to one appearing in a *PA* cumulated index) describes each article listed under a key term.

Beginning the search with *aggressive behavior,* we find no listing for that term in the Subject Index (*SA,* Vol. 24, 1976). Instead, as illustrated in Figure 5–H, we find an entry for "Aggression" (**38**) and two variants (i.e., Aggressive, Aggressiveness). Several references appear in that entry. The descriptive phrase "adolescent aggression & rebellion due to parental practices" (**39**) suggests that this reference may be relevant. If we had searched the Subject Index with the terms "Adolescents" (**40**) or "Parent" (**41**), we would have found the same phrase (**39**). Following the identifying phrase is a citation

FIGURE 5–H
Subject Index entries from *Sociological Abstracts: Cumulative Subject Index* (Vol. 24, pp. 1318, 1319, 1385), 1976.

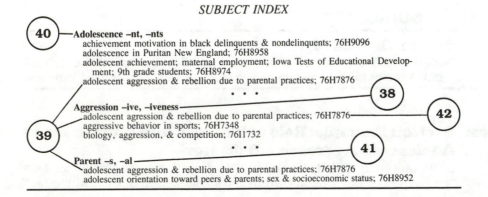

SUBJECT INDEX

(40) ──Adolescence –nt, –nts
   achievement motivation in black delinquents & nondelinquents; 76H9096
   adolescence in Puritan New England; 76H8958
   adolescent achievement; maternal employment; Iowa Tests of Educational Development; 9th grade students; 76H8974
   adolescent aggression & rebellion due to parental practices; 76H7876
   · · · (38)

   Aggression –ive, –iveness──
   adolescent agression & rebellion due to parental practices; 76H7876──(42)
   aggressive behavior in sports; 76H7348
(39)   biology, aggression, & competition; 76I1732
   · · · (41)

   Parent –s, –al──
   adolescent aggression & rebellion due to parental practices; 76H7876
   adolescent orientation toward peers & parents; sex & socioeconomic status; 76H8952

FIGURE 5—I

A partial main entry citation from the "Adolescence and Youth" section in *Sociological Abstracts*, April 1976, 24(1), 193.

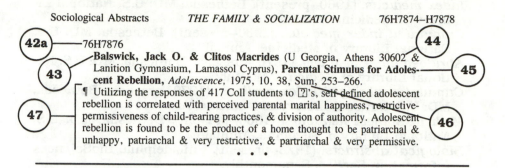

Sociological Abstracts   *THE FAMILY & SOCIALIZATION*   76H7874–H7878

(42a) ——76H7876

Balswick, Jack O. & Clitos Macrides (U Georgia, Athens 30602 & Lanition Gymnasium, Lamassol Cyprus), **Parental Stimulus for Adolescent Rebellion,** *Adolescence,* 1975, 10, 38, Sum, 253–266.

¶ Utilizing the responses of 417 Coll students to ☐'s, self-defined adolescent rebellion is correlated with perceived parental marital happiness, restrictive-permissiveness of child-rearing practices, & division of authority. Adolescent rebellion is found to be the product of a home thought to be patriarchal & unhappy, patriarchal & very restrictive, & partriarchal & very permissive.

• • •

number (**42**), which we use to locate the reference in the main entry section of the corresponding volume of *SA*.

As shown in Figure 5—I, each entry in the main entry section begins with the citation number (**42a**), followed by the name(s) of the author(s) (**43**), the institutional affiliation(s) of the author(s) (**44**), and the article title (**45**). Bibliographic information provided (**46**) includes the journal title, the year of publication, the volume and the issue numbers, the month or date of issue, and the page numbers. In addition, an abstract (**47**) summarizes the article.

The Source Index, arranged by journal title, indicates the availability of articles from selected journal titles through a reproduction service offered by the publisher, Sociological Abstracts, Inc. Occasionally copies of papers presented at scholarly conferences, abstracted in *SA* supplements, are also available. This index is important because many conference papers are unpublished and would be difficult to locate without this service.

4 Medicine and the Life Sciences

Sources Discussed

Index medicus. (1960–present). Bethesda, MD: U.S. National Library of Medicine. Monthly.

Cumulated index medicus. (1960–present). Bethesda, MD: U.S. National Library of Medicine. Annual.

Abridged index medicus. (1970–present). Bethesda, MD: U.S. National Library of Medicine. Monthly.

Cumulated abridged index medicus. (1970–present). Bethesda, MD: U.S. National Library of Medicine. Annual.

Medical subject headings. (1960–present). Bethesda, MD: U.S. National Library of Medicine. Annual.

Biological abstracts. (1926–present). Philadelphia: BioSciences Information Service. Semimonthly.

Serial sources for the BIOSIS data base. (1978–present). Philadelphia: BioSciences Information Service. Annual.

Section Example: Split-Brain Phenomena and Epilepsy

W. S. Sahakian (1979) briefly discusses research on split-brain phenomena within the context of organic mental disorders. He notes that "humans, unlike animals, can function despite severance of the two hemispheres" of the brain (p. 395). Surgeons have discovered that severing the corpus callosum, nerve fibers connecting brain hemispheres, results in reduction of epileptic seizures. Since this topic concerns a medical procedure, we should consult biomedical literature. This topic may be represented by the search terms *epilepsy* and *corpus callosum.*

Index Medicus

Index Medicus provides coverage of over 2500 serial publications worldwide. Monthly issues are cumulated annually in *Cumulated Index Medicus.* For smaller libraries, *Abridged Index Medicus* has listings for more than 100 English-language journals and is cumulated annually as *Cumulated Abridged Index Medicus.*

We begin our search by consulting *Medical Subject Headings* (*MeSH*) to verify that our search terms correspond to subject headings, which are illustrated in Figure 5–J. Acceptable subject headings are printed in large boldface type, whereas unacceptable terms appear in small type. Figure 5–J lists several subject headings, the most general of which is "Epilepsy" (**48**). Related terms are identified by cross references (**49**). For explanations of other notations, see the "Introduction" to *MeSH.*

In the *Index,* both citations and subheadings appear following the term "Epilepsy" (see Figure 5–K). The subheading "Surgery" (**50**) is a logical subgroup for the topic. A relevant article for our purpose is "Division of the corpus callosum for uncontrollable epilepsy" (**51**) by D. H. Wilson and others (**52**). The entry provides complete bibliographic information including the journal title, the place of publication, the volume number, the issue number (in parentheses), journal page numbers, and the date of publication (**53**). Because journal

FIGURE 5–J
Subject headings from *Medical Subject Headings (MeSH)* (p. 144), 1982.

(48)——————EPILEPSY
　　　　　　C10.228.140.490+

　　　　　　see related
　　　　　　　　KINDLING (NEUROLOGY)
(49)——————XR CONVULSIONS

　　　　　　EPILEPSY, ABDOMINAL see EPILEPSY, TEMPORAL LOBE

　　　　　　EPILEPSY, FOCAL
　　　　　　C10.228.140.490.207+
　　　　　　77; was indexed under JACKSONIAN SEIZURE 1970–76
　　　　　　X　EPILEPSY, PARTIAL

　　　　　　EPILEPSY, GRAND MAL
　　　　　　C10.228.140.490.234.225
　　　　　　　　　　　• • •

　　　　　　EPILEPSY, PETIT MAL
　　　　　　C10.228.140.490.234.270
　　　　　　X　ABSENCE
　　　　　　X　AKINETIC PETIT MAL
　　　　　　X　PYKNOLEPSY

FIGURE 5–K
Citations on epilepsy from the Subject Index of *Cumulated Index Medicus* (Vol. 19, Book 9, pp. 6857, 6861).

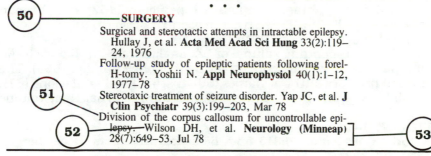

1978　　　　**CUMULATED INDEX MEDICUS**　　　　EPILEPSY

EPILEPSY
Macrosomy, precocious puberty, severe oligophrenia and epilepsy in a boy born of consanguineous parents. Guazzi GC, et al. **Acta Neurol (Napoli)** 33(1):31–43, Jan–Feb 78
Delivery complicated by myasthenia gravis and epilepsy. Hansson U, et al. **Acta Obstet Gynecol Scand** 57(2):183–5, 1978
　　　　• • •
(50)——————**SURGERY**
Surgical and stereotactic attempts in intractable epilepsy. Hullay J, et al. **Acta Med Acad Sci Hung** 33(2):119–24, 1976
Follow-up study of epileptic patients following forel-H-tomy. Yoshii N. **Appl Neurophysiol** 40(1):1–12, 1977–78
(51) Stereotaxic treatment of seizure disorder. Yap JC, et al. **J Clin Psychiatr** 39(3):199–203, Mar 78
(52) Division of the corpus callosum for uncontrollable epilepsy. Wilson DH, et al. **Neurology (Minneap)** 28(7):649–53, Jul 78 **(53)**

titles are frequently abbreviated, for complete titles you should consult the list of indexed journals, published in the January issue of *Index Medicus* and reprinted annually in *Cumulated Index Medicus.*

Biological Abstracts

Biological Abstracts (*BA*) indexes research in more than 8000 journals, proceedings, and symposia published worldwide. Although *BA* has several indexes, we will describe the Subject Index, published twice a month and cumulated twice a year. For each publication

FIGURE 5–L
Subject Index entries illustrating the Subject Keyword Index of *Biological Abstracts Semiannual Cumulative Index* (Vol. 70, pp. 1493, 1766), July–December 1980.

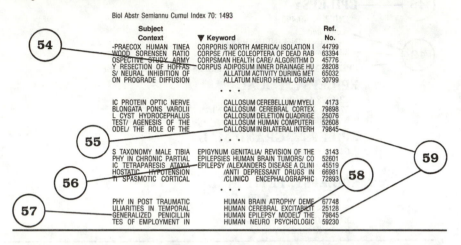

entry, a subject word-string composed of two parts is constructed: selected significant words from the article's abstract indicating major aspects of the study and words derived from the article's title. A citation is represented in the Subject Index by an entry for each significant word (keyword) in the string.

In Figure 5–L, excerpts from *BA* Subject Index, Volume 70, illustrate this alphabetically arranged keyword index. "Corpus" (**54**) appears as a keyword with several entries referring to the "corpus callosum" (**55**). Although the string of keywords is incomplete, the remaining words of each entry (to the left and right of "corpus callosum") provide some indication of the content of the article cited. A second index entry appears for the keyword "Epilepsy" (**56**) and is qualified by the phrases "generalized penicillin" (**57**) and "human epilepsy model" (**58**). These two index entries refer to the same citation, reference number 79845 (**59**).

In the corresponding volume of *BA*, as illustrated in Figure 5–M, citations are arranged sequentially by reference number (**59a**). The citation provides authors' names (**60**), institutional affiliations (**61**), and bibliographic information (**62**) including journal title, volume

FIGURE 5–M
A portion of citation 79845 from *Biological Abstracts*, December 15, 1980, *70*(12), 8332.

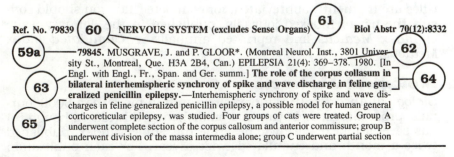

number, issue number (in parentheses), page numbers, and year of publication. The article title (**64**) appears in boldface type, preceded by a language note (**63**) and followed by an abstract (**65**).

References

Bandura, A., & Walters, R. (1963). *Social learning and personality development.* New York: Holt, Rinehart & Winston.

Biehler, R. F. (1978). *Psychology applied to teaching* (3rd ed.). Boston: Houghton Mifflin.

Kahn, R. L. (1974). Conflict, ambiguity and overload: Three elements in job stress. In A. McLean (Ed.), *Occupational stress* (pp. 47–61). Springfield, IL: Charles C Thomas.

Kahn, R. L., Wolfe, D. M., Quinn, R. P., Snoek, J. D., & Rosenthal, R. A. (1964). *Organizational stress: Studies in role conflict and ambiguity.* New York: Wiley.

McDavid, J. W., & Harari, H. (1974). *Psychology and social behavior.* New York: Harper & Row.

Rambo, W. W. (1982). *Work and organizational behavior.* New York: Holt, Rinehart & Winston.

Rosenthal, R., & Jacobson, L. (1968) *Pygmalion in the classroom.* New York: Holt, Rinehart & Winston.

Sahakian, W. S. (Ed.). (1979). *Psychopathology today: The current status of abnormal psychology* (2nd ed.). Itasca, IL: Peacock.

U.S. Department of Health, Education & Welfare (HEW). (1967). *1967 annual report* (SuDoc FSI.1:967). Washington, DC: U.S. Government Printing Office.

6 The Author/Citation Approach to Searching

Sources Discussed

Social sciences citation index (SSCI). (1969–present). Philadelphia: Institute for Scientific Information. Three times a year. Cumulated annually and quinquenially (1966–1970, 1971–1975).

Science citation index (SCI). (1961, 1964–present). Philadelphia: Institute for Scientific Information. Bimonthly. Cumulated annually and quinquennially (1965–1969, 1970–1974, 1975–1979).

Why Citation Searching?

Original contributions to a field occur as authors report a new finding or offer a new theory that significantly changes understanding of a field, points researchers in a new direction, or initiates a new area of investigation. The learned-helplessness research discussed in chapter 4 provides an example of such contributions. However, a new line of published research may exist for years without being described by appropriate subject headings in a subject-oriented indexing or abstracting service. Subject indexers may use a variety of indexing terms to identify publications in an emerging area of study. Thus, using a subject search to identify sources relevant to a topic may be difficult.

The citation-searching approach provides you with an alternative to subject searching. To search for citations, you do not need to rely on subject headings, indexing terms, or the judgment of indexers. Citation indexes are based on the premise that published research in an area includes references to previously published papers, which provide the theoretical and empirical context for the new paper. And this premise is based on the assumption that researchers are familiar with the literature in their area and have selected and cited previously published references that are relevant to their own work. If you can identify an important early source in an area, you should be able to identify later articles citing that source.

Chapter Example: Impact of John Garcia's Bright-Noisy-Water Research on Psychology

In the 1950s and 1960s, John Garcia and his colleagues conducted a series of studies investigating the effects of radiation on living organisms. Rats were exposed to a variety of stimuli, including x-radiation, shock, loud noises, saccharin-flavored water, salt-flavored water, and so forth. Eventually Garcia challenged Pavlov's assertion that any formerly neutral stimulus could be made to elicit a reflex response through classical conditioning. He asserted that certain neurological or biological limitations in various species prohibited these species from learning certain associations (Wortman & Loftus, 1981, pp. 149–152). Some psychologists have called this finding the Garcia effect (Smith, Sarason, & Sarason, 1982). In one study, known as the "bright-noisy-water experiment," this limitation on learning was demonstrated. Rats learned avoidance of bright-noisy water paired with shock and of saccharin-flavored water paired with illness. The rats, however, failed to learn to avoid saccharin-flavored water paired with shock and bright-noisy water paired with illness (Garcia & Koelling, 1966). These results, as well as related findings by Garcia and others, were later used by Seligman (1970) in support of the general notion of "preparedness of an organism for learning" (p. 408), or what some might call biological capacity. An interesting research question might be, "What impact has Garcia's bright-noisy-water research had on other areas of psychology?"

Social Sciences Citation Index® *(SSCI)*

Initiated in 1969, *SSCI* currently provides complete coverage of about 1500 journals and selective coverage of approximately 2800 additional journals in the social sciences. It includes disciplines from anthropology, archaeology, business, and communication to psychology, sociology, statistics, and urban planning; and it lists articles, editorials, letters, book reviews, conference reports, conference proceedings, and books. *SSCI* does not, however, provide abstracts or detailed contents of the sources covered.

The "General Introduction" to *SSCI* claims that the index can be used to answer such questions as the following: "Has this paper been cited?" "Has there been a review on this subject?" "Has this work been extended?" "Who else is working in this field?" "Has this theory been applied to a new field?" (*SSCI*, 1981, p. 9). Published three times per year and cumulated annually and quinquennially, *SSCI* contains four basic parts: the Citation Index, the Source Index, the Corporate Index, and the Permuterm Subject Index. A typical *SSCI* annual cumulation is composed of several thousand pages in multiple volumes. A companion series, begun in 1963, is *Science Citation Index* (*SCI*), which covers literature in the natural sciences.

Using *SSCI*

Searching with *SSCI* begins with an accurate citation to an important early primary source. In our search, the complete citation is "Relation of Cue to Consequence in Avoidance Learning" by John Garcia and Robert Koelling, *Psychonomic Science*, 1966, Volume 4, pages 123–124. For the purpose of illustration we begin with a recent annual cumulation of *SSCI*. As the search progresses, we both work backward in time to earlier volumes and check unaccumulated recent issues.

We turn first to the Citation Index in *SSCI*. This section is arranged alphabetically by cited author. If an author has more than one citation, the entries are listed below his or her name chronologically by year of publication. Figure 6–A presents a segment of the 1980 *SSCI* annual cumulation showing entries for the first author, John Garcia (**1**). Scanning the list, we find "*66 PSYCHON SCI 4 123*" (**2**), an abbreviated citation

FIGURE 6–A
Entries in the Citation Index of the *Social Sciences Citation Index*® *1980 Annual* (Vol. 1, cols. 4622, 4623), 1981, showing recently published articles that have referred to an earlier source by J. Garcia.

Citation Index

		VOL	PG	YR
(1) GARCIA J				
57 J COMPARATIVE PHYSIO 50 180				
INGRAM DK	EXP AGING R	6	113	80
61 PSYCHOL REV 68 383				
ARCHER T	PHYSL PSYCH	8	40	80
• • •				
(2) 66 PSYCHON SCI 4 123				**(3)**
SEE SCI FOR 7	ADDITIONAL CITATIONS			
ARCHER T	PHYSL PSYCH	8	40	80
"	Q J EXP PSY	32	197	80
• • •				
(4) DAVIS WJ	J COMP PHYS	138	157	80
DELPRATO DJ	BEHAV THER	11	79	80
ELKINS RL	DRUG AL DEP	5	101	80
GASTON KE	BEHAV NEUR	28	129	80

in italics to the original reference, including (in order) the year of publication, the journal title, the volume number, and the number of the first page of the article. The note "SEE SCI FOR 7 ADDITIONAL CITATIONS" (3) indicates that *Science Citation Index* (*SCI*) contains seven other references that are not included in *SSCI*. Following this information, in alphabetical order by author, is a list of sources included in this edition of *SSCI* that have cited the Garcia and Koelling (1966) reference. The article by R. L. Elkins (4) appearing in the journal *Drug and Alcohol Dependence* (DRUG AL DEP), Volume 5, starting on page 101 in the year 1980, seems interesting.

To learn more about the Elkins reference, we turn to the Source Index of *SSCI*, illustrated in Figure 6–B. Listed in this index are all of the articles, books, and other documents included in the 1980 edition, arranged in alphabetical order by author. We find R. L. Elkins (4a) listed in Volume 3, on page 2850. Then we locate the entry for DRUG AL DEP (5). The title of the article that appears in this journal is listed above (6), and it indicates that the article extends Garcia's research to treatment of alcoholics. The citation further elaborates on the information we obtained from the Citation Index: Elkins's article appears in the second issue of Volume 5 (7) of the journal *Drug and Alcohol Dependence*, is

FIGURE 6–B

Entries in the Source Index of *Social Sciences Citation Index 1980 Annual Cumulation* (Vol. 3, col. 2850), 1981, providing complete bibliographic information on recently published articles by R. L. Elkins, including the earlier sources referenced.

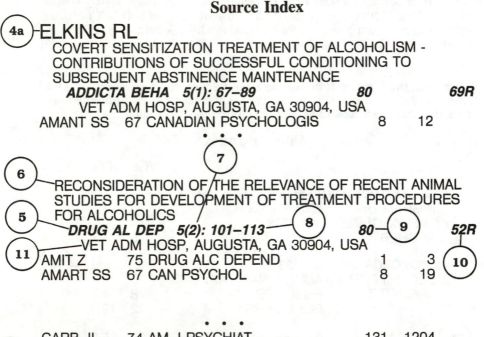

Source Index

(4a) ELKINS RL
  COVERT SENSITIZATION TREATMENT OF ALCOHOLISM -
  CONTRIBUTIONS OF SUCCESSFUL CONDITIONING TO
  SUBSEQUENT ABSTINENCE MAINTENANCE
    ADDICTA BEHA 5(1): 67–89   80   69R
      VET ADM HOSP, AUGUSTA, GA 30904, USA
    AMANT SS   67 CANADIAN PSYCHOLOGIS   8   12
                      • • •
                    (7)
(6) RECONSIDERATION OF THE RELEVANCE OF RECENT ANIMAL
    STUDIES FOR DEVELOPMENT OF TREATMENT PROCEDURES
(5) FOR ALCOHOLICS
    DRUG AL DEP 5(2): 101–113 (8)   80 (9)   52R
      VET ADM HOSP, AUGUSTA, GA 30904, USA
(11) AMIT Z   75 DRUG ALC DEPEND   1   3 (10)
     AMART SS   67 CAN PSYCHOL   8   19

                      • • •
    GARB JL   74 AM J PSYCHIAT   131   1204
(2a) GARCIA J   66 PSYCHON SCI   4   123
       "   68 COMMUNICATIONS BEH A   1   389
     GREEN KF   71 SCIENCE   173   749

13 pages long (8), was published in 1980 (9), and includes a total of 52 references (10). The citation also indicates Elkins's address at the time this article was published (11). Following this information, in alphabetical order by author, is a list of the 52 sources cited by Elkins in this article. Part of the way down the list is the Garcia and Koelling (1966) article (2a) with which we began.

If you were to expand this search, you might include related articles by Garcia listed in the Citation Index. You would have to consult both previous and later editions of *SSCI* for references published in other years.

Other Features of *SSCI*

The Permuterm® Subject Index is a relatively new feature, providing a kind of subject access to *SSCI* materials. Unlike other indexes we have examined, this index does not depend upon the judgment of professional indexers or upon a controlled vocabulary. Generated and produced by computer, it lists as subject entries significant words in article titles. Entries for the Elkins article would, therefore, appear under "animal studies" and "alcoholics" in the permuterm index. A subject search with this index may be useful if you are interested in a broad range of publications from many social science disciplines. However, if an article's title does not accurately indicate its subject content, you might overlook the article. Furthermore, the Permuterm Subject Index does not identify related articles. Therefore you could not use it to uncover the relation between the Elkins and Garcia articles that we found using the author/citation approach.

The Corporate Index contains two sections—geographic and organizational. Citations in this index are arranged by the organizational locations of the authors and their institutional affiliations. For example, knowing (from the *SSCI* Source Index) that Elkins was at the Veterans Administration Hospital in Augusta, Georgia, when, his article was published, you might wish to learn what other research has been reported by persons at that institution.

The List of Source Publications includes both the full title and the abbreviation for each journal covered in an edition of *SSCI*. The list is included in each cumulation of *SSCI*. We used it to decipher the abbreviations PSYCHON SCI and DRUG AL DEP. You should consult the list for the accurate, complete title or the appropriate abbreviation for each journal identified. Because more than 4000 different journals are indexed in each edition of *SSCI*, abbreviations for many journals are similar. Attempting to locate an incorrect journal title can be time-consuming and frustrating.

Each annual edition of *SSCI* includes an extensive "General Introduction," which provides further information about many features of *SSCI* and *SCI*. The introduction also includes historical information on the development of citation indexing, research on citation indexing, and research on patterns of scientific citation.

Incidentally, *SSCI* and *SCI* are extremely expensive indexes. Although they provide unique coverage of literature in the social and natural sciences, they are too expensive for many smaller libraries. Thus, to use this tool, you may need to visit a library other than the one you usually use. A reference librarian may be able to help you identify libraries that have this tool.

References

Garcia, J., & Koelling, R. A. (1966). Relation of cue to consequence in avoidance learning. *Psychonomic Science, 4,* 123–124.

Seligman, M. E. P. (1970). On the generality of the laws of learning. *Psychological Review, 77,* 406–418.

Smith, R. E., Sarason, I. G., & Sarason, B. R. (1982). *Psychology: The frontiers of behavior* (2nd ed.). New York: Harper & Row.

Social sciences citation index [SSCI] 1980 Annual. (1981). Philadelphia: Institute for Scientific Information.

Wortman, C., & Loftus, E. (1981). *Psychology.* New York: Knopf.

7 Government Publications

Sources Discussed

U.S. Superintendent of Documents. (1895–present). *Monthly catalog of United States government publications.* Washington, DC: U.S. Government Printing Office. Monthly.

Index to U.S. government periodicals. (1970–present). Chicago: Infordata International. Quarterly; cumulated annually.

Library of Congress, Exchange and Gifts Division. (1910–present). *Monthly checklist of state publications.* Washington, DC: U.S. Government Printing Office. Monthly.

National Technical Information Service. *Government reports announcements & index.* (1946–present). Springfield, VA: National Technical Information Service. Bimonthly.

United Nations, Dag Hammarskjold Library. (1950–present). *UNDOC: Current index; United Nations document index.* New York: United Nations. Monthly.

What Are Government Publications?

Government publications include materials issued by local, state, regional, federal, foreign, or international governmental organizations. Issuing agencies may be part of an executive, legislative, or judicial branch, or they may be independent regulatory agencies. Publications are produced in every size from a single page to a multi-volume set and are available on almost any topic imaginable.

In this chapter we focus attention primarily upon publications of the United States federal government. These publications are the most widely distributed and available throughout the United States. The federal government, through the U.S. Government Printing Office (GPO), is the largest single publisher in the United States. In 1981 the GPO operated government bookstores in 26 cities around the United States and distributed 28 million publications to 1353 depository libraries (U.S. GPO, 1982). In 1980 over 2 million orders for sales were processed, approximately 135 million publications were distributed, and over 52 thousand documents were cataloged (U.S. GPO, 1981).

State, local, and international publications are less widely distributed and less accessible. Therefore we mention them briefly.

We cover government publications in a separate chapter for several reasons. The vast majority of publications issued by government bodies are **not** covered by the various abstracting and indexing services discussed in chapters 4, 5, and 6. A variety of separate indexes provide access to government publications. Also, many libraries having a sizable collection of government publications handle these materials separately from other library materials.

The Depository Library Program

More than 1300 college, university, government, special, and public libraries in the United States have been designated as Federal Depository libraries. Depositories are eligible to receive more than 3,800 classes of publications free of charge. These libraries are operated according to provisions of the *Guidelines for the Depository Library System* (U.S. GPO, 1978).

Each federal congressional district is eligible for two depository libraries designated by members of the House, and each state may contain one or two others designated by senators (U.S. GPO, 1978). According to the *Guidelines,*

the purpose of depository libraries is to make U.S. Government publications easily accessible to the public and to insure their continued availability in the future. . . . Depository libraries will receive free Federal public documents. . . . Each depository should select frequently used and potentially useful materials appropriate to the objectives of the library. Each library should acquire and maintain the basic catalogs, guides and indexes, retrospective and current, considered essential to the reference use of the collection. . . . Libraries shall make depository publications available for the free use of the general public. (U.S. GPO, 1978, pp. 1–7)

Depository libraries receive, on a daily basis, shipments of publications in any series that they have requested.

Nondepository libraries and individuals may purchase numerous federal government publications. These publications may be ordered from sources such as the following: *U.S. Government Books,* published bimonthly and listing about 1000 publications in each issue; *Subject Bibliographies,* listing federal government publications in over 300 different areas such as alcoholism, child abuse, family planning, juvenile delinquency, mental health, occupational safety, reading, vocational education, and women; and the *Monthly Catalog,* which we discuss in this chapter.

Chapter Example: Aging

In this chapter we consider psychology-related publications on the subject of aging. Since the early 1970s, life-span developmental psychology and gerontology have become areas of increasing importance to psychologists. At the same time, numerous federal agencies have generated a wealth of relevant information on aging. The most important questions at this point are: How are the publications of the federal agencies organized? How can people interested in topics covered by the agencies locate these publications?

Organization of Government Publications

Many nondepository libraries order, receive, catalog, and arrange government publications in the same way they do materials from commercial publishers. For example, nondepository libraries may catalog and shelve government monographs with other books, government periodicals with other library periodicals, and selected materials of special importance with the general library collection. Depository libraries receive so many government publications, however, that these libraries handle such publications separately from other library materials.

Most depository libraries organize documents according to the Superintendent of Documents Classification number system (SuDoc). The SuDoc system is an alpha-numeric notation system. Let us examine the SuDoc number for a typical publication, *Policy Issues for the Elderly Poor* (SuDoc number CSA 1.9:6172-8), issued by the Community Services Agency. Table 7–A explains this SuDoc number. The letters at the beginning indicate the parent department or agency. Departments and agencies are subdivided into bureaus, offices, and agencies, indicated by numbers. Particular publi-

TABLE 7–A

Analysis of a Superintendent of Documents Classification System (SuDoc) Number

	Symbol	Designation	Hierarchy
Class stem	CSA	parent agency	Community Services Administration
	1	subagency	Office of Policy Planning and Evaluation
	.9	series	C.S.A. Pamphlet Series
Book number	:6172-8	publication	*Policy Issues for the Elderly Poor*

TABLE 7–B

Organization of Issuing-Agency Prefix Codes for Selected Agencies in the Superintendent of Documents (SuDoc) Classification System

SuDoc Code	Agency
CR	Civil Rights Commission
CSA	Community Services Agency
ED	Department of Education
HE	Department of Health & Human Services (formerly HEW)
HE3	Social Security Administration
HE20	Public Health Service
HE20.2000	National Institutes of Health
HE20.8100	National Institute of Mental Health
HE22	Health Care Financing Administration
HE23	Office of Human Development Services
HE23.3000	Administration on Aging
HH	Department of Housing & Urban Development
L	Department of Labor

cation series are identified following a decimal point. A colon then precedes the number identifying the particular publication.

In the SuDoc system, as illustrated in Table 7–B, publications are organized by issuing agency. (Notice from that table that there are several agencies of potential interest to psychologists.) Thus two publications on the same topic by different agencies would be located in different places, whereas two publications on radically different topics by the same agency might be located together. Within this organization publications are arranged in alpha-numeric order. This system is difficult to manage partly because the federal government is extremely large and partly because governmental reorganization changes the numbering system. For example, educational materials have been issued by the Education Bureau in the Interior Department (code I16), transferred to the Federal Security Agency (code of FS), which became the Department of Health, Education and Welfare (code HE). More recently a separate cabinet-level Department of Education was created (code ED), and the Reagan administration is considering another reorganization. Thus, to avoid confusion and to locate relevant publications, you must rely on indexes.

Monthly Catalog of United States Government Publications

The primary index to federal government publications is the *Monthly Catalog of United States Government Publications (Monthly Catalog)* issued by the U.S. Superintendent of Documents. First issued in 1895, this index has since endured several changes of title and structure. In 1976 the *Monthly Catalog* adopted its present format. Currently, cataloging and indexing follow the same rules that the Library of Congress uses in cataloging books (see chapter 3). Prior to 1976, the *Monthly Catalog* used its own

FIGURE 7–A
Subject Index entries for publications on aging from the *Monthly Catalog of U.S. Government Publications* (pp. I-214, I-227), September 1981.

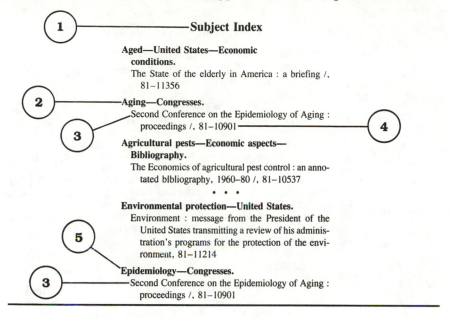

system, which many librarians believe was incomplete and difficult to use.

Each issue of the *Monthly Catalog* contains a description of new documents processed during that monthly period. There are six monthly indexes—author, title, subject, series/report, stock number, and title key word. Some are cumulated semiannually and annually. Each year a special *Serials Supplement*, listing publications issued three or more times a year, is published.

Using the *Monthly Catalog*

Searching for publications on aging provides an illustration of use of the *Monthly Catalog*. Figure 7–A presents several Subject Index (1) entries from the September 1981 issue. Although there are no publications indexed in September 1981 under the general subject heading "Aging," the more specific subject subdivision "Aging—Congresses" (2) is of interest. Listed here is the publication "Second Conference on the Epidemiology of Aging" (3), entry number 81–10901 (4). If we also search under the subject heading "Epidemiology" (5) in this *Monthly Catalog* issue, we would locate the same publication, entry 81–10901. This number includes the year of cataloging (81) and a number that indicates a particular item (10901).

To learn more about this item, you turn to the body of the *Monthly Catalog*. Here publications are arranged alphabetically by agency in each issue. Entries are numbered sequentially within each annual volume, beginning with entry 1 in January of each year. Entry 81–10901 is shown in Figure 7–B. The boldface heading for the National Institute on Aging (6) precedes all entries for this agency. Document descriptions begin with the entry number (4a). The SuDoc

FIGURE 7–B
Information provided for government publications included in the *Monthly Catalog of U.S. Government Publications* (p. 57), September 1981.

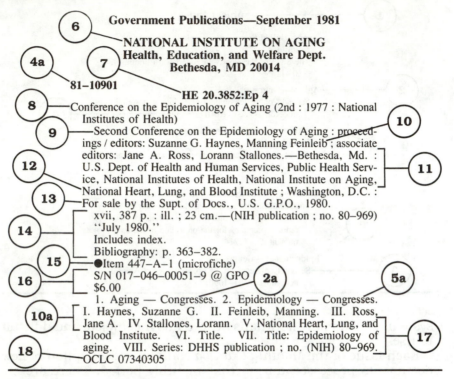

number (**7**), essential for locating the publication in a depository library, is HE20.3852:Ep4. The publication is listed in the *Monthly Catalog* under the Main Entry (**8**), which indicates that this was a conference held in 1977, sponsored by the National Institutes of Health (NIH). The full title, *Second Conference . . . Aging* (**9**), informs us that it was the second NIH conference on the epidemiology of aging. Conference proceedings were edited by four individuals, Haynes, Feinlieb, Ross, and Stallones (**10**) and were published in Bethesda, Maryland, by the National Institute on Aging (**11**). The National Heart, Lung, and Blood Institute (**12**) provided assistance. The volume was published in 1980 and can be purchased from the Superintendent of Documents (**13**).

Descriptive notes indicate that this document contains 387 pages of text with illustrations and is part of the National Institutes of Health Publication Series. It also contains an index and an extensive (20-page) bibliography (**14**). It is sent to depository libraries selecting this series as Item 447-A-1 (**15**) in paper copy or microfiche, and it may be purchased for $6.00 for each copy from GPO as stock number S/N 017-046-00051-9 (**16**).

Following this information are tracings (see chapter 3), which indicate all the ways this document is indexed. As we discovered previously the document is entered in the Subject Index under "Aging" (**2a**) and "Epidemiology" (**5a**). The Author Index contains entries for each of the editors (**10a**). Additional index entries enable you to lo-

FIGURE 7–C

Index entries for publication 81–10901 from the *Monthly Catalog of U.S. Government Publications* (pp. I-208, I-156, I-278), September 1981, showing the full title entry in the Title Index, an editor entry in the Author Index, and two entries in the Title Keyword Index.

Title Index

(**9a**)

Science and technology of low speed and motorless
  flight : proceedings of a symposium /, 81–11078
Second Conference on the Epidemiology of Aging :
  proceedings /, 81–10901
Section 504 resources manual /, 81–10874
Services for children of alcoholics : symposium, September 24–26, 1979, Silver Spring, Maryland /,
  81–10931

Author Index

(**10b**)

Federal Judicial Center. cn
  Disqualification of federal judges by peremptory
  challenge /, 81–11020
Feinleib, Manning.
  Second Conference on the Epidemiology of Aging :
  proceedings /, 81–10901
Feld, I. L. (Ignatz L.)
  Comminution by the attrition grinding process /,
  81–10975

Title Keyword Index

(**19**)

agency equal employment opportunity public informa	**81-11300**
agents guide to forfeiture of assets /, Drug	**81-11016**
Aging :proceedings /, Second Conference on the Epi	**81-10901**
" ., Improving the future of	**81-10953**
agreement :. Review United States-Japan rice	**81-11359**

• • •

(**20**)

environments /, An impedance technique for determi	**81-11063**
EPA) /, Livermore regional air quality (LIRAQ) mod	**81-10708**
epidemiological and clinical research (1967–1979)	**81-10926**
Epidemiology of Aging :proceedings /, Second Confe	**81-10901**
equal employment opportunity public information ma	**81-11300**
Equality, Development and Peace, Copenhagen, Denma	**81-11145**

cate this book by agency, by title and abbreviated title, and by publication series (**17**). Because, since 1976, cataloging and indexing have been done with the computerized systems of the Online Computer Library Center (OCLC), the *Monthly Catalog* also provides this reference (**18**).

Figure 7–C illustrates several of the index entries. In the Title Index entry 81–10901 appears under its full title (**9a**) and in the Author Index it appears under each editor's name, here under editor Feinleib (**10b**). A new feature of the *Monthly Catalog*, initiated in 1980, is the Title Keyword Index. This index lists entries under important words selected from the document title and is similar in structure to the *Biological Abstracts* subject index. In this index, publication 81–10901 appears under the key words "Aging" (**19**) and "Epidemiology" (**20**).

To develop an effective subject-search strategy you begin with relevant descriptors in the most recent issues of the Subject and Title Keyword indexes and work backward in time to older volumes. Because prior to 1976 the *Monthly Catalog* used its own list of subject-indexing terms, your challenge is to identify terms under which relevant publications were indexed. Subject-indexing terms for publications on aging have included *aged, elderly, gerontology, old age, older Americans,* and *senior citizens.* Cumulated indexes are available for the periods 1951–1960, 1961–1965, 1966–1970, 1971–1976, and 1900–1971. Their main emphasis is on subject indexing.

Continuing a search on aging would uncover numerous additional publications. Several illustrations of what you might find are presented in Table 7–C. For each sample publication, the SuDoc number, the issuing agency, and the title are listed.

U.S. Government Periodicals

Agencies of the federal government issue over a thousand different periodicals. These publications are not indexed in the *Monthly Catalog,* and many are not covered in the indexing or abstracting services discussed elsewhere in this book. The *Index to U.S. Government Periodicals,* published quarterly and cumulated annually, covers a selection of these materials. In 1981 this computer-generated index provided access to 182 federal government periodicals by author and subject. At present, the earliest available volume covers materials published in 1970.

Figure 7–D shows several entries on aging from the 1981 Index. One article of possible interest is "Assessment of behavioral changes in geriatric patients" (**21**), written by J. Richard Wittenborn (**22**). It appeared in the quarterly journal, *Psychopharmacology Bulletin,* Volume 17, issue 4, on pages 96–103, in October, 1981 (**23**). To order a copy of the article you would use the microfiche identifying number, 091. To decipher any abbreviations in the entry you should check the key to abbreviations printed in the front of each volume.

There are many federal government periodicals that may be of interest to psychologists. These include *Aging, American Education, Children Today, Monthly Labor Review, Schizophrenia Bulletin,* and *Social Security Bulletin.*

Other Sources

Materials discussed in the remainder of the chapter may be unavailable in many libraries. We note these sources, however, to complete our discussion and to give you an idea of the variety of publications in existence.

State documents. Agencies in each state in the United States issue a variety of publications. Few libraries have large collections of anything other than their own state's publications. The source that provides the most comprehensive coverage of these materials is the *Monthly Checklist of State Publications,* compiled by the Library of Congress. Published monthly for more than 70 years (with annual indexes), the *Checklist* provides a record of state documents received at the Library of Congress. The checklist depends on the goodwill and cooperation of many state agencies, which voluntarily

TABLE 7–C

Sampling of the Publications on Aging Issued by Various Federal Agencies

SuDoc Number	Issuing Agency	Publication Title
C3.186 :P23/85	Census Bureau	Social & Economic Characteristics of the Older Population: 1978. (1979)
E3.26/4 :0220	Energy Department	A Comparison of Energy Expenditures by Elderly & Non-Elderly Households—1975 & 1985. (1980)
HE1.202 :So1	Administration on Aging	Evaluative Research on Social Programs for the Elderly. (1977)
HE20.3714 :2	National Inst. of Health	Teaching of Chronic Illness & Aging. (1975)
HH1.2 :L95/3	Housing & Urban Development Dept.	Low Rise Housing for Older People: Behavioral Criteria for Design. (1977)
J1.8/2 :Se5	Law Enforcement Assistance Adm.	Crime Prevention Handbook for Senior Citizens. (1977)
Y4.Ag4 :R8/3/pt.1	Special Committee on Aging, Senate	The Nation's Rural Elderly. Hearings. Pt. 1 Winterset, IA (1976)
Y4.Ag4/2 :Ag4/8	Select Committee on Aging, House	Future Directions for Aging Policy: A Human Services Model. Report. (1980)
Y4.Ag4/2 :E12/27	Select Committee on Aging, House	Elder Abuse (An Examination of a Hidden Problem). Staff Report. (1981)

FIGURE 7–D
Listings for publications on aging in the *Index to U.S. Government Periodicals* (p. 30), 1981.

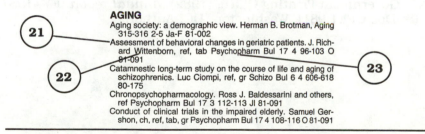

INDEX TO U.S. GOVERNMENT PERIODICALS

AGING
Aging society: a demographic view. Herman B. Brotman, Aging 315-316 2-5 Ja-F 81-002
Assessment of behavioral changes in geriatric patients. J. Richard Wittenborn, ref, tab Psychopharm Bul 17 4 96-103 O 81-091
Catamnestic long-term study on the course of life and aging of schizophrenics. Luc Ciompi, ref, gr Schizo Bul 6 4 606-618 80-175
Chronopsychopharmacology. Ross J. Baldessarini and others, ref Psychopharm Bul 17 3 112-113 Jl 81-091
Conduct of clinical trials in the impaired elderly. Samuel Gershon, ch, ref, tab, gr Psychopharm Bul 17 4 108-116 O 81-091

forward materials to the Library of Congress. Consequently, it is not a complete list of all state publications. Some states also issue their own checklists.

Unpublished technical reports. Each year thousands of research, development, and technical reports are written. Many of these are prepared under requirements of grants or contracts with federal government agencies; others are prepared for state or local governmental agencies. Similar to materials included in ERIC's *RIE* (see chapter 5), these reports are often reproduced and distributed in a limited fashion. The National Technical Information Service (NTIS) indexes and abstracts them in *Government Reports Announcements and Index*.

United Nations publications. These publications are indexed in *UNDOC: Current Index*, prepared by the Dag Hammarskjold Library. This index is issued 10 times a year, with annual cumulations and indexes. Like the U.S. federal government, the United Nations issues thousands of reports annually. As in the case of state documents and technical reports, however, these publications are often difficult to obtain.

Further information. Given the limitations of space available in this chapter, we have covered only the most highly visible sources and those that we judge to be most widely available in college libraries. For additional information you should consult a reference librarian or government documents librarian. If you are interested in exploring this area further, the best general guidebook with which we are familiar is Morehead's (1978) *Introduction to United States Public Documents*. Other sources that you may find useful are Andriot's (1982) *Guide to U.S. Government Publications* and Palic's (1975) *Government Publications: A Guide to Bibliographic Tools*.

References

Andriot, J. L. (Ed.). (1982). *Guide to U.S. government publications* (Vol. 1). McLean, VA: Documents Index.

Morehead, J. (1978). *Introduction to United States public documents* (2nd ed.). Littleton, CO: Libraries Unlimited.

Palic, V. M. (1975). *Government publications: A guide to bibliographic tools* (4th ed.). Washington, DC: Library of Congress.

U.S. Government Printing Office. (1978). *Guidelines for the Depository Library System as adopted by the Depository Library Council October 18, 1977* (SuDoc GPI.23/4:D44/978). Washington, DC: Author.

U.S. Government Printing Office. (1981). *Annual report, FY–1980* (SuDoc GPI.1:980). Washington, DC: Author.

U.S. Government Printing Office. (1982). *Annual report, FY–1981* (SuDoc GPI.1.981). Washington, DC: Author.

8 The Computer Search

Sources Discussed

Thesaurus of psychological index terms (3rd ed.). (1982). Washington, DC: American Psychological Association.

Information industry market place: An international directory of information products and services. (1981). New York: Bowker.

Rationale for a Computer Search

We have discussed a variety of bibliographic tools for the identification of psychological literature. These tools cover a broad range of disciplines: psychology, sociology, management, education, biology, medicine, and so forth. Searching the many tools relevant to a particular topic can be time-consuming, especially if the topic is related to two or more fields and if two or more indexes provide useful citations. A search may be particularly difficult if it involves a topic combining two, three, or more concepts. If you are faced with such a complex multifaceted search, your task may be eased by the use of a computer.

Many indexes and abstracting services have been produced by computers. Increasingly, publishers are making the computer records from which their print indexes are produced available for searching via computer terminals. This service, commonly called on-line bibliographic searching, allows the researcher to bypass the cumbersome task of manually searching printed indexes. The result of a computer search is a list of citations to literature that is tailored to your particular research topic.

Most computer searches are done by a librarian experienced in the use of computer databases. Search results can be improved, however, if you understand what the computer can accomplish. In this chapter we focus on selecting a relevant database from those available, structuring a search, and learning what to expect from a computer search. Finally, in the event that this service is not available to you, we discuss other possible sources of computer searches.

Selecting a Database

Table 8–A lists selected databases of possible interest to psychologists. Included in the table are information on the name and producer of each database, the subject areas covered by each database, the years for which each database is available (as of early 1983), and the name of the corresponding print index, if one is available. These are **bibliographic** databases, meaning that a search of them yields citations to journal articles, books, dissertations, government reports, and other documents.

The databases listed cover various subject areas. Those, such as ERIC, previously mentioned as print-index equivalents will be familiar; others, such as Drug Info/Alcohol Use and Abuse, have no print equivalent. The only way in which these unpublished databases can be searched is by computer.

Most publishers began producing indexes from computer databases in the late 1960s or early 1970s, and few publishers have included citations from earlier years. Only two databases listed in Table 8–A contain citations earlier than 1960. For this reason, print indexes and abstracts are essential to supplement a computer search for complete coverage of a topic.

Chapter Example: Effects of Auditory or Visual Stimulation on Tonic Immobility in Birds

Selecting search terms is essentially the same whether you conduct a manual or a computer search. You must identify key words, terms,

TABLE 8–A Selected Databases in Psychology

Database	Producer	Subject Areas	Dates Available[a]	Print Equivalents
		Behavioral Sciences		
ABI/INFORM	Data Courier, Inc.	Business and management	1971+	None
Child Abuse and Neglect	National Center on Child Abuse and Neglect	Child abuse	1965+	*Child Abuse and Neglect*
Drug Info/Alcohol Use and Abuse	Drug Information Services, University of Minnesota	Psychological or sociological aspects of drug and alcohol abuse	1968+	None
ERIC	Educational Resources Information Center	Education	1966+	*Research/Resources in Education* *Current Index to Journals in Education*
Family Resources Database	National Council on Family Relations	Marriage and the family	1970+	No exact equivalent
Language and Language Behavior Abstracts	Sociological Abstracts, Inc.	Linguistics and language	1973+	*Language and Language Behavior Abstracts*
Management Contents	Management Contents, Inc.	Business and management	1974+	*Management Contents*
NARIC	National Rehabilitation Information Center	Rehabilitation of the physically or mentally disabled	1950+	None

Table continued

[a]The plus sign (+) in this column means "to the present."

(Table 8-A continued)

Database	Producer	Subject Areas	Dates Available[a]	Print Equivalents
NIMH Database	National Clearinghouse for Mental Health Information	Mental health	1969–1981	No exact equivalent
PsycINFO	American Psychological Association	Psychology	1967+	*Psychological Abstracts,* plus 25% more citations after 1980
Social SciSearch	Institute for Scientific Information	Social sciences	1972+	*Social Sciences Citation Index*
Sociological Abstracts	Sociological Abstracts, Inc.	Sociology	1963+	*Sociological Abstracts*
Sciences				
BIOSIS Previews	BioSciences Information Service	Biology and the life sciences	1969+	*Biological Abstracts* *Biological Abstracts/RRM*
MEDLINE	National Library of Medicine	Biomedicine	1966+	*Index Medicus* *Index to Dental Literature* *International Nursing Index*
SciSearch	Institute for Scientific Information	Sciences	1974+	*Science Citation Index*
Multidisciplinary				
Comprehensive Dissertation Index	University Microfilms International	Doctoral dissertations and masters theses reproduced by UMI	1861+	*Comprehensive Dissertation Index*
GPO Monthly Catalog	Government Printing Office	Unclassified government documents	1976+	*Monthly Catalog of United States Government Publications*

[a]The plus sign (+) in this column means "to the present."

and authors of relevant research (review chapters 2, 3, and 4). You should consult a thesaurus, if available, in this process (see chapters 3, 4, and 5).

We have selected the topic "effects of auditory or visual stimulation on tonic immobility in birds" to illustrate a computer-search strategy. M. R. Denny (1980) describes tonic immobility as a secondary defense mechanism used by many animal species against predators; animals using this defense are more likely to escape a predator's grasp if they become acquiescent or immobile than if they do not. Since its first identification, tonic immobility has been called "fascination, . . . catalepsy, thanatosis, enhancement, rho, akinesis, paroxysmal inhabitation, Totsell reflex, mesmerism, fright paralysis, monoidism, bewitchment, death feign or sham, animal hypnosis, and immobility reaction" (Denny, 1980, p. 408). Research has indicated that some humans exhibit similar behaviors; for example, rape victims reporting an incident-induced paralysis (Suarez & Gallup, 1979).

We have also selected the PsycINFO database, which is roughly the equivalent of *Psychological Abstracts* and which uses the *Thesaurus of Psychological Index Terms* as its source of controlled vocabulary (see chapter 4 for details). Unlike *Psychological Abstracts*, however, the PsycINFO database includes citations, such as doctoral dissertations, that no longer appear in the print indexes.

The specific topic (effects of auditory or visual stimulation on tonic immobility in birds) contains three separate concepts: auditory or visual stimulation, tonic immobility, and birds (as a specific subject population). Each concept represents one set of descriptors and citations—citations on auditory or visual stimulation, citations on tonic immobility, and citations on birds. If we searched the print indexes, we would find a few relevant references listed under each of these topics. We would, however, also find a much larger number of irrelevant sources. For example, using the subject term *auditory or visual stimulation,* we would identify many sources. But a large proportion would deal with populations other than that of birds (e.g., rats, cats, primates). Additionally, most probably would not be concerned with tonic immobility. Only citations that deal with all three concepts are relevant to this topic. The search process should thus be a subset composed by the intersection (symbolized ∩) of these three larger sets. The Venn diagram in Figure 8–A contains a pictorial representation of this logical structure.

Once you have outlined the general structure of a search, you must identify specific search terms for each concept. Using the Relationship Section of the *Thesaurus,* we find descriptors for *tonic immobility, auditory stimulation, visual stimulation,* and *birds.* There are broader, narrower, and related terms listed under *auditory stimulation* and *visual stimulation;* but no terms appear directly relevant to the topic. Under *birds* are listed twelve narrower terms representing specific species of birds. Articles concerning any of these species might be relevant, so you would probably want to include in the *birds* set of subject terms all of the narrower terms listed.

Although *tonic immobility* is used as a subject heading in the *Thesaurus,* its broader (*motor processes*) and related (*alarm responses* and *animal defensive behavior*) terms are much less pre-

FIGURE 8–A

A Venn diagram showing intersection (∩) of three sets of concepts to yield a subset of highly relevant documents.

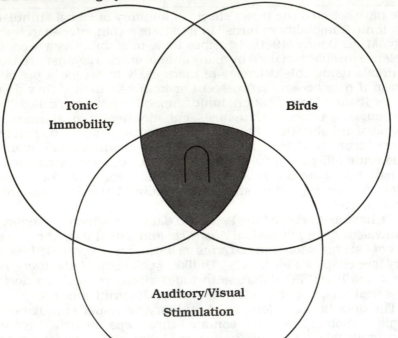

TABLE 8–B

Computer-Search Terms From Three Concept Sets

Concept	Computer Search Terms	
Tonic Immobility	tonic immobility[a,b]	paroxysmal[a]
	death feign[a]	inhibition[a]
	animal hypnosis[a]	Totstell reflex[a]
	fascination[a]	mesmerism[a]
	catalepsy[a]	fright paralysis[a]
	thanatosis[a]	monoidism[a]
	enhancement[a]	bewitchment[a]
	rho[a]	death sham[a]
	akinesis[a]	immobility reaction[a]
Auditory/Visual Stimulation	auditory stimulation	visual stimulation
Subject Population	birds	ducks
	blackbirds	geese
	budgerigars	penguins
	canaries	pigeons
	chickens	quails
	doves	robins
	sea gulls	

[a]Non-*Thesaurus*, free-text terms.
[b]*Tonic immobility* has also been a descriptor in the *Thesaurus* since 1978.

cise and appear irrelevant to this search. The entry in the *Thesaurus* also shows that *tonic immobility* was included in the controlled vocabulary only after 1978.

An advantage of most computer searches is that they are not limited to the controlled vocabulary of a thesaurus. Through **free-text searching** (searching words and phrases as they appear in the text of an abstract, a title, and so forth), relevant terms that may not appear in a thesaurus can be searched. Thus some of the synonyms provided in Denny's (1980) description might be included as search terms; for example, *death feign, animal hypnosis, fascination,* and *catalepsy.*

Table 8–B presents revised and enlarged sets of search terms for the topic we selected. In a search, the computer would typically be instructed first to collect citations indexed under each concept, for example, all citations on *birds* or its related terms. Then the computer would be instructed to combine the three sets, identifying only those citations that contain at least one descriptor or term from each of the three concept groups. The result is a subset of relevant bibliographic citations.

You can further restrict a computer search in several ways. You can exclude documents published in a language that you cannot read. Perhaps you would like to limit the search to publications within a particular period of time, such as the last 5 years. You might want to exclude particular types of publications, such as dissertations.

Search Results

Figure 8–B presents a *Psychological Abstracts* citation with its equivalent PsycINFO computer-generated citation. (Please note: The format of the computer-generated citation may vary slightly depending upon the search service used.) One difference between the two citations is that the abstract number in the computer-generated citation (**1a**) includes the number of the *PA* volume in which the printed citation appears (**1**). The name(s) of the author(s) (**2; 2a**), the institutional affiliation(s) (**3; 3a**), the title (**4; 4a**), the bibliographic information (**5; 5a**), and the abstract (**6; 6a**) are identical. The computer-generated citation contains information not included in the *PA* print version.

Appended to the computer citation (**7a**) is the brief descriptive phrase that identifies this article in the subject index (**7**). The computer citation may also contain the language of publication (**8**), the year of publication (**9**), the publication type (**10**), and a list of descriptors used to index the document (**11**).

Sources of Computer-Search Services

Many college and university libraries offer on-line bibliographic searching as a service of their reference or public-services department. Some libraries make this service available to all members of the academic community, whereas others may restrict it to faculty members. Some libraries do not charge for the service, others charge a nominal fee (from $3.00 to $10.00 per search), and others expect the requester to bear the full cost of the computer search (often $25.00 or more). A librarian or a pamphlet on the services

FIGURE 8–B

Entry from *Psychological Abstracts*, August 1981, *66*(2), (on the left) with the corresponding subject-access entry from the semiannual *Subject Index* (p. 987), July–December 1981. On the right is the citation as it appears in the PsycINFO database.

EXPERIMENTAL PSYCHOLOGY (ANIMAL) 66: 2935-2944

(2)

(1)

(3)

(5)

2938. **Rovee-Collier, Carolyn; Kaufman, Lynn W. & Farina, Phillip.** (Rutgers U, Douglass Coll, New Brunswick) The critical cues for diurnal death feigning in young chicks: A functional analysis. *American Journal of Psychology*, 1980(Jun), Vol 93(2), 259–268.—Assessed the critical determinants of extended diurnal death feigning in a refinement experiment in which visual and tactile cues during rearing and/or testing were systematically eliminated. 95 domestic Leghorn chicks were reared in either a social environment or physical (tactile) isolation, and half in each rearing condition were reared and/or tested under conditions of visual restriction. As expected, social rearing was a prerequisite of the manifestation of extended death feigning; however, the incidence and duration of death feigning was attenuated by functional visual isolation of socially reared chicks during either rearing or testing. It is concluded that visual novelty of the environment is the minimal condition for sustained death feigning by young chicks in the daylight hours. (23 ref)—*Journal abstract*.

(4)

(6)

SUBJECT INDEX

Tonic Immobility

(7) social rearing vs physical & visual isolation, diurnal death feigning, chicks, 2938

(1a)

(4a) 66–02938 Vol No: 66 Abstract No: 02938

(2a) The critical cues for diurnal death feigning in young chicks: A functional analysis.
Rovee-Collier, Carolyn K.; Kaufman, Lynn W.; Farina, Phillip

(9)

(3a) Rutgers U, Douglass Coll, New Brunswick
American Journal of Psychology 1980 Jun Vol 93(2) 259–268

(10)

(5a) Language: ENGLISH Document Type: JOURNAL ARTICLE

(8) Assessed the critical determinants of extended diurnal death feigning in a refinement experiment in which visual and tactile cues during rearing and/or testing were systematically eliminated. 95 domestic Leghorn chicks were reared in either a social environment or physical (tactile) isolation, and half in each rearing condition were reared and/or tested under conditions of visual restriction. As expected, social rearing was a prerequisite of the manifestation of extended death feigning; however, the incidence and duration of death feigning was attenuated by functional visual isolation of socially reared chicks during either rearing or testing. It is concluded that visual novelty of the environment is the minimal condition for sustained death feigning by young chicks in the daylight hours. (23 ref)

(6a)

(11) Descriptors: CHICKENS, ANIMAL ENVIRONMENTS, SOCIAL ISOLATION, ISOLATION EFFECT, CUES, TONIC IMMOBILITY, VISUAL STIMULATION

(7a) Identifiers: social rearing vs physical & visual isolation, diurnal death feigning, chicks

offered by your library can inform you of the availability of these services on your campus.

If this service is not available in your library, a reference librarian may be able to provide advice on obtaining a computer search. You may be able to obtain assistance from another library in your geographic region. If you are willing to pay for a computer search, you may wish to investigate a professional service. One such service is PASAR, part of the Psychological Abstracts Information Service, which performs retrospective searches of the PsycINFO database on a full cost-recovery basis. Request forms are available in each monthly issue of *PA*. Searches are also available through companies that provide information commercially and have access to a broad range of databases. Before placing a search request, obtain an estimate of the cost; be prepared to spend at least $30.00 for a computer search. For further information, consult a recent copy of *Information Industry Market Place*.

References

Denny, M. R. (Ed.). (1980). *Comparative psychology: An evolutionary analysis of animal behavior.* New York: Wiley.

Suarez, S. D., & Gallup, G. G. (1979). Tonic immobility as a response to rape in humans: A theoretical note. *Psychological Record, 29,* 315–320.

9 Psychological Tests and Measures

Sources Discussed

Buros, O. K. (Ed.). *Mental measurements yearbook* (*MMY*). Highland Park, NJ: Gryphon Press.
  (1938). *1938 Mental measurements yearbook* (*First MMY*)
  (1972). *Seventh MMY.*
  (1978). *Eighth MMY* (2 vols.).
Buros, O. K. (Ed.). (1961). *Tests in print* (*TIP*). Highland Park, NJ: Gryphon Press.
Buros, O. K. (Ed.). (1974) *Tests in print II* (*TIP2*). Highland Park, NJ: Gryphon Press.
Goldman, B. A., & Saunders, J. L. (Eds.). (1974). *Directory of unpublished experimental mental measures* (Vol. 1). New York: Behavioral Publications.
Goldman, B. A. & Busch, J. C. (Eds.). (1978, 1982). *Directory of unpublished experimental mental measures* (Vols. 2–3). New York: Human Sciences Press.
Educational Testing Service, Test Collection. (1975–present). *Tests in microfiche.* Princeton, NJ: Author. Annual.

Need for Information on Tests

There are many situations in which a psychologist may need information about a psychological test. For example, school psychologists evaluate children referred by classroom teachers who suspect learning disabilities. The school psychologist must know which of the many tests available are most appropriate to ascertain whether a learning disability exists and, if so, what its nature and its severity are. A vocational counselor uses tests to gather information about interests, aptitudes, and skills to advise people regarding career options. He or she must know which tests are best for which kinds of career-counseling situations. A researcher may use tests to measure attitudes, behaviors, abilities, or other variables relevant to a particular research hypothesis. The researcher might construct a new measuring instrument or use one that already exists. A new measure may lack reliability or validity and may not allow comparison with prior research. Thus the researcher will want to know about existing tests and measures appropriate to the particular research situation.

There exist various situations in which you, as a student, may need information about psychological tests. You may be enrolled in a course in tests and measurements in which you are required to investigate a variety of psychological tests. You may be designing a research project and need to select or devise a relevant test or other measuring instrument. You may be writing a paper on a topic that relies heavily on research involving the use of one or several particular tests or measures. As such, you may need to understand thoroughly the assumptions, theoretical and empirical structure, and mechanics of the measures used in that research.

Psychological tests or measures of one type or another are used in most research in psychology. Tests and measures represent particular ways of observing and gathering information about psychological concepts. A psychological concept, such as personality, may be operationally defined in many ways.

Different operational definitions of the same psychological concept may lead to different measurement strategies. For example, a researcher has many options when deciding how to measure personality. Two very different strategies for the measurement of personality might involve, on the one hand, the use of a structured, objective personality inventory such as the *Minnesota Multiphasic Personality Inventory* (Hathaway & McKinley, 1970) or, on the other hand, the use of a less structured, projective personality test such as the *Rorschach Inkblot Test* (Rorschach, 1942). These two tests were developed in different ways, they involve radically different measurement strategies, and they yield different kinds of information about personality. As a result, the selection of one test may lead to research findings that are at odds with the findings resulting from another test selection. For this reason, the decision to use a particular test in the design of a study will have a critical impact on the findings that emerge from the research. As a researcher, you must be aware of the influence of differing measurement strategies on the research that you conduct. As a reader of the research of others, you must be aware of these same issues in order to understand and compare intelligently the findings of studies employing dissimilar measurement strategies. To develop this awareness, you must locate information on the test(s) under consideration.

Thousands of tests have been created. For purposes of locating them, they may be grouped in two general classes: published tests and unpublished tests. Published tests may be purchased by psychologists from commercial test-publishers, such as the Consulting Psychologists Press, the Educational Testing Service, and the Psychological Corporation. Many published tests are heavily used and are therefore readily available. In contrast, unpublished tests and measures are not available from commercial publishers. They may be less well known to psychologists and used less frequently by them. The primary application of unpublished tests is in research, and such tests may be mentioned or described in only one or a few research reports.

In this chapter, we discuss sources of information about psychological tests and measures. We focus attention first on published tests and then on unpublished tests.

Published Tests

The most extensive coverage of published standardized tests commercially available in the English-speaking world is provided by the *Mental Measurements Yearbooks* (*MMY*) and their companion publications, compiled and edited by Oscar Krisen Buros, with the assistance of Luella Buros. In all, eight *MMYs* have been published from 1938 through 1978. The *MMY* volumes provide detailed factual information on published tests and critical reviews of most of those tests. Additionally, the volumes provide extensive bibliographies of more than 77,000 references to tests listed in *MMY* as well as lists and reviews of books on testing and measurement. The eight *MMY* editions supplement each other, with succeeding editions including only new tests, substantially revised tests, or new information about previously reviewed tests.

A related source, also compiled and edited by O. K. Buros, is *Tests in Print* (*TIP*), published in 1961. This was followed in 1974 by *Tests in Print II* (*TIP2*). *TIP* and *TIP2* contain information that supplements material included in the *First MMY* through the *Seventh MMY*. *TIP* includes a list of tests that were out of print (no longer available from commercial publishers) as of 1961; *TIP2* supplements this information with a list of additional tests out of print as of 1974. *TIP2* provides a cumulative index to 2467 tests and other materials reviewed in the first seven *MMYs*. *TIP2* also contains information on 471 new and revised tests that appeared after publication of the *Seventh MMY* but that were not included in the *Eighth MMY*.

The *Eighth MMY* covers 1184 new or revised tests issued during the period of 1971 through 1977. It contains 898 original reviews for 638 tests, 140 reviews excerpted from journals for 96 tests, and a bibliography of 576 books on testing (Buros, 1978).

In addition to the eight *MMYs*, *TIP*, and *TIP2*, Buros has published numerous monographs containing information in particular areas. These monographs are intended for the psychologist who does not need the complete coverage of all topics provided by *MMY*. They are similar in form and content to *MMY* and cover the areas of personality, reading, intelligence, and so forth.

Using the *Mental Measurements Yearbook* (*MMY*)

To illustrate how to use *MMY*, we have selected the general area of personality testing. We wish to examine a test developed within the theoretical framework of Henry Murray's (1938) conception of personality. One possibility is the *Thematic Apperception Test* (*TAT*) developed by Murray and his colleagues at the Harvard Psychological Clinic (Murray, 1971). The *TAT*, however, is a projective test that requires a great deal of training and experience to administer, score, and interpret. For this reason, we decided not to pursue the *TAT*. Instead, we sought a structured, objective personality test. By checking Anne Anastasi's (1982) book on testing, we located the *Edwards Personal Preference Schedule* (*EPPS*) (Edwards, 1959). However, the *EPPS* has not been revised in more than thirty years. Searching for a more recent test, we again checked Anastasi (1982), which indicates that the *Jackson Personality Inventory* (*JPI*) is a structured, objective personality test. The *JPI*, conceptualized within the framework of Murray's personality theory, is a recently developed test. For information about the *JPI* we begin by examining the most recent edition of the *MMY*.

The *Eighth MMY* contains six indexes—Index of Test Titles, Index of Names, Scanning Index, Index of Book Titles, Periodical Directory and Index, and Publishers Directory and Index. The *Jackson Personality Inventory* (*JPI*) is listed as test entry-number 593 in the alphabetically arranged Index of Test Titles. The *JPI* is also listed alphabetically under the name of its author, D. N. Jackson, in the Index of Names, and alphabetically under *JPI* in the Personality Section of the Scanning Index. Had we not known about the *JPI*, we could have consulted the Scanning Index and found information about numerous personality tests, selecting one that suited our purposes.

For information about the *JPI*, you would turn to test entry 593 in the Tests and Reviews section of the *Eighth MMY*. Tests are arranged by type; for example, achievement batteries, personality tests, and so forth. Each test in each edition of *MMY* is provided with a sequential entry number. Every test entry follows the same general format, illustrated in Figure 9–A for the *JPI*, and each test description begins with the test entry number (1). The star (2) indicates that the *JPI* is a new test not previously included in *MMY*, *TIP*, or *TIP2*. The test title (3) appears in boldface print, followed by information on the groups for which the test is intended (4), the date of copyright or publication (5), the title acronym (6), subscales for which test scores are available (7), brief factual notes about the test (8), forms included in the test and age or grade levels available (9), machine-scorable answer sheets available (10), cost (11), administration time (12), the author (13), and the publisher (14). The asterisk (15) at the end of this description indicates that the information was compiled after an examination of the actual test materials. The entry may also provide information on scoring services and other details. Following the descriptive information is a list of references (16) to materials concerning the development, evaluation, and use of the test. Next is a critical review of the test (17), which begins with the name and position of the reviewer. Two reviews are provided for the *JPI*, extending from page 867 through page 873 of the *Eighth MMY*.

FIGURE 9–A

Portions of a review of a test from O. K. Buros (Ed.), (1978), *Eighth Mental Measurements Yearbook* (Vol. 1, p. 878).

<u>867</u>]   TESTS & REVIEWS: PERSONALITY   <u>593</u>

[593]

★**Jackson Personality Inventory.** Grades 10–16 and adults; 1976; JPI; 16 scores: anxiety, breadth of interest, complexity, conformity, energy level, innovation, interpersonal affect, organization, responsibility, risk taking, self esteem, social adroitness, social participation, tolerance, value orthodoxy, infrequency; norms consist of means and standard deviations only for high school students; in addition, linear transformations and normal-curve-based estimates of percentile ranks are presented for college students; 1 form (7 pages); manual (38 pages); reliability data (2 pages); profile (2 pages); separate answer sheets must be used; $16.50 per set of 10 tests, 25 answer sheets and profiles, scoring stencil, and manual; $11 per 25 tests; $2.75 per 25 answer sheets; $3 per scoring stencil; $2.75 per 25 profiles; $5.50 per manual; postage extra; specimen set not available; (40–50) minutes; Douglas N. Jackson; Research Psychologists Press, Inc.*

REFERENCES

1. CREEGGAN, SHEILA MOREEN. *Factors Affecting Faculty Attitudes Toward Curriculum Change in Selected Diploma Schools of Nursing.* Master's thesis, University of Western Ontario (London, Ont., Canada), 1970.
2. MORF, MARTIN E.; KAVANAUGH, ROBERT D.; and McCONVILLE, MARC. "Intratest and Sex Differences on a Portable Rod-and-Frame Test." *Percept & Motor Skills* 32(3):727–33 Je '71.* (*PA* 47:2001)
3. JACKSON, DOUGLAS N.; HOURANY, LARRY; and VIDMAR, NEIL J. "A Four-Dimensional Interpretation of Risk Taking." *J Personality* 40(3):483–501 S '72.* (*PA* 50:1081)
4. GARDNER, R. C. "Ethnic Stereotypes: The Traditional Approach, a New Look." *Can Psychologist* 14(2):133–48 Ap '73.* (*PA* 51:979)
5. JACKSON, DOUGLAS N. "The Relative Validity of Scales Prepared by Naive Item Writers and Those Based on Empirical Methods of Personality Scale Construction." *Ed & Psychol Meas* 35(2):361–70 su '75.* (*PA* 54:8701)
6. JACKSON, DOUGLAS N. "Reliability of the Jackson Personality Inventory." *Psychol Rep* 40(2):613–4 Ap '77.*

LEWIS R. GOLDBERG, *Professor of Psychology, University of Oregon; and Director, Institute for the Measurement of Personality; Eugene, Oregon.*
Psychometrics has been severely buffeted of late. The past decade has witnessed a barrage of invective against the employment of psychological tests, culminating in a spate of nonnegotiable demands for test moratoria. The popularity of courses in assessment has slipped dramatically, and most graduate students now consider psychometric knowledge as desirable as unspiked fruit punch. Even purely scientific investigators of personality structure have been lambasted, and their efforts

Information Sources for Unpublished Tests

Thousands of tests, questionnaires, and other measuring instruments created by researchers are not commercially available. Often they have been mentioned only briefly in a research report or presented in an article or book. You may find locating such measuring instruments difficult. Information on their technical adequacy (reliability, validity, norms, and so forth) may be scanty, if available at all. Since the 1960s, several sources that attempt to provide access to these varied materials have been published.

The *Directory of Unpublished Mental Measures* supplements *MMY* by listing unpublished tests appearing in a large number of psychology and related journals. At present there are three volumes of the *Directory*, covering tests available in journal articles published in 1970 (Vol. 1), 1971–1972 (Vol. 2), and 1973–1974 (Vol. 3). As of Spring 1983, Volume 4 is in preparation. Included in the *Directory* is a brief description of each measure and a reference to the journal in which the test and related information appeared. Tests are grouped by general type (attitude, personality, and so forth), and a subject index is included.

Tests in Microfiche is a current source that provides information on unpublished research instruments. Since 1975, this publication has been issued annually by the Educational Testing Service. Each edition covers 50 to 100 tests and questionnaires identified from various sources such as conference programs. Included in this service are microfiche copies of the tests, brief descriptive information about the tests, and an annual annotated index.

Several other sources provide information of possible interest. In *Measures for Psychological Assessment*, K. Chun, S. Cobb, and J. R. P. French (1975) compiled 3,000 references to articles in social science journals that reported the use of various tests and measures. *The Sourcebook of Mental Health Measures* (Comrey, Backer, & Glaser, 1973) complements their efforts by listing and abstracting 1,100 tests, questionnaires, rating scales, and inventories not included by Chun, Cobb, and French. *Tests and Measurements in Child Development* (Johnson, 1976; Johnson & Bommarito, 1976), limited to research on children, provides a more focused approach. *Handbook I* (Johnson & Bommarito, 1976) covers tests reported prior to 1976 for infants through children 12 years old. *Handbook II* (Johnson, 1976) expands the coverage to infancy through age 18 and includes materials reported from 1966 through 1974. Descriptive information is provided for each measure, accompanied by the source of the information.

Several sources exist in the area of attitude measurement. A three-volume series published by the Survey Research Center at the University of Michigan (Robinson, Athanasiou, & Head, 1969; Robinson, Rusk, & Head, 1968; Robinson & Shaver, 1973) covers approximately 300 attitude scales. These volumes provide descriptive information, brief evaluative information, the source, and either sample items or the whole measure. M. E. Shaw and J. M. Wright (1967) present approximately 175 attitude measurement scales, including the full text, scoring, and background information.

Together these sources supplement *MMY* by providing information on a wide variety of unpublished measures. One final source of possible interest, *Women and Women's Issues* (Beere, 1979), is a recent compilation of information concerning 235 instruments. It includes information about both unpublished and published measures made available through the end of 1977.

Using these sources, you can search for information about tests and measures relevant to your research, your papers, and your courses. One cautionary note, however: Because of the sensitivity of some published psychological tests and measures, you may not find the measures themselves in your college library. Indeed, some libraries, as a matter of policy, do not maintain a collection of psychological tests. Instead, in many cases, you will need to contact a psychologist in a department of psychology, counseling center, or other facility at your college to discuss the availability of a test you wish to examine.

References

Anastasi, A. (1982) *Psychological testing* (5th ed.). New York: Macmillan.

Beere, C. A. (1979). *Women and women's issues: A handbook of tests and measures.* San Francisco: Jossey-Bass.

Buros, O. K. (Ed.). (1978). *Eighth Mental Measurements Yearbook.* Highland Park, NJ: Gryphon Press.

Chun, K. Cobb, S., & French, J. R. P. (1975). *Measures for psychological assessment.* Ann Arbor, MI: Survey Research Center.

Comrey, A. L., Backer, T. E., & Glaser, E. M. (1973). *A sourcebook of mental health measures.* Los Angeles: Prepared for the National Institute of Mental Health by the Human Interaction Research Institute.

Edwards, A. L. (1959). *Edwards Personal Preference Schedule Manual,* Revised 1959. New York: The Psychological Corporation.

Hathaway, S. R., & McKinley, J. C. (1970). *Booklet for the Minnesota Multiphasic Personality Inventory.* New York: The Psychological Corporation.

Johnson, O. G. (Ed.) (1976). *Tests and measurements in child development: Handbook II* (2 vols.). San Francisco: Jossey-Bass.

Johnson, O. G., & Bommarito, J. W. (Eds.) (1976). *Tests and measurements in child development: Handbook I.* San Francisco: Jossey-Bass.

Murray, H. A. (1938). *Explorations in personality: A clinical and experimental study of fifty men of college age.* New York: Oxford University Press.

Murray, H. A. (1971). *Thematic Apperception Test Manual.* Cambridge, MA: Harvard University Press.

Robinson, J. P., Athanasiou, R., & Head, K. B. (1969). *Measures of occupational attitudes and occupational characteristics.* Ann Arbor, MI: Survey Research Center.

Robinson, J. P., Rusk, J. G., & Head, K. B. (1968). *Measures of political attitudes.* Ann Arbor, MI: Survey Research Center.

Robinson, J. P., & Shaver, P. R. (1973). *Measures of social psychological attitudes.* Ann Arbor, MI: Survey Research Center.

Rorschach, H. (1942). *Psychodiagnostics: A diagnostic test based on perception.* (Trans. P. Lemkau & B. Kronenburg) Berne: Huber. (1st German ed., 1921; U.S. distributor, Grune & Stratton)

Shaw, M. E., & Wright, J. M. (1967). *Scales for the measurement of attitudes.* New York: McGraw-Hill.

10 Miscellaneous Sources: Current-Awareness Services, Biographical Information, and Book Reviews

In previous chapters, we have presented various sources useful for pursuing information on a topic in psychology. The purpose of tools such as *Annual Review of Psychology*, *Psychological Abstracts*, and *Social Sciences Citation Index* is to construct a retrospective literature review consisting of citations to sources relevant to a topic.

The tools discussed in this chapter serve quite a different purpose. They can broaden your knowledge of a particular area of research. For example, current-awareness tools update a retrospective literature search already undertaken and may identify new directions in research or persons conducting such research. Biographical information on a prominent researcher or author may lend his or her thesis support based on information such as academic credentials or current research interests. Book reviews provide informed opinions to help you identify the potential usefulness and reliability of books in the field. Thus the tools presented in this chapter may supplement your knowledge of a given research area.

1 Current-Awareness Services

Sources Discussed

Current contents: Social & behavioral sciences. (1969–present).
   Philadelphia: Institute for Scientific Information. Weekly.
American Psychological Association. (1981–present). *PsycSCAN:*
   Applied psychology. Washington, DC: Author. Quarterly.
American Psychological Association. (1980–present). *PsycSCAN:*
   Clinical psychology. Washington, DC: Author. Quarterly.
American Psychological Association. (1980–present). *PsycSCAN:*
   Developmental psychology. Washington, DC: Author. Quarterly.
American Psychological Association. (1982–present). *PsycSCAN:*
   LD/MR. Washington, DC: Author. Quarterly.

The well-read psychologist may identify many journals in which major, interesting studies are routinely published. Unfortunately, he or she often cannot afford a subscription to each journal of interest. Current-awareness tools help the researcher keep abreast of recently published research. The previously mentioned indexing tools, such as *PA*, are preferred for retrospective literature searching because they provide a comprehensive list of sources relevant to a topic and include extensive indexes. In contrast, current-awareness services usually do not provide detailed indexing. But they supplement retrospective literature review by offering two important conveniences. First, they provide timely access to journal literature because, in some cases, they can be produced more quickly than indexing tools can. Second, the researcher can quickly scan the contents of those journals that he or she has identified as regularly containing articles of interest or on topics under investigation.

One such tool, *Current Contents: Social & Behavioral Sciences* (*CC*), reproduces the tables of contents from about 1,300 journals in the social and behavioral sciences around the world. Each journal issue's table of contents provides article titles, authors' names, and the page number on which each article begins. Because of the production process employed, *CC* is extremely timely: Issues of *CC* are compiled and sent to subscribers weekly. Thus, within a few weeks of the publication of a journal article, the *CC* reader is made aware of the article's availability. In addition to providing timely access to journal contents, *CC* allows the researcher to browse the contents of many journal issues of possible interest. The journals included are grouped under broad subject areas, such as education, psychology, and psychiatry, allowing the user to browse by subject areas.

Each weekly issue of *CC* also contains an author index and a brief subject index. The latter is constructed from significant words appearing in article titles. It is important to note that, if you want to use *CC* effectively, you must be familiar with journal titles that routinely publish articles on your topic and you must be willing to scan *CC* regularly.

In conjunction with *CC*, the Institute for Scientific Information also provides a service called OATS® (Original Article Text Service). For a fee, this service will provide copies of articles covered in *CC*. Information on the service is provided in each issue of *CC*.

A similar series is *PsycSCAN*, published quarterly by the American Psychological Association. Whereas *CC* provides access to journals representing a wide range of disciplines, *PsycSCAN* limits coverage to journals of potential interest to psychologists. Presently there are four separate *PsycSCAN* publications, each covering a select set of journals in a particular subject area: *Applied Psychology*, *Clinical Psychology*, *Developmental Psychology*, and *Learning Disabilities/ Mental Retardation*. Although not as timely as *CC*, this series has several advantages. A researcher can subscribe to one source that provides coverage in a particular area of interest. Each journal-article entry in *PsycSCAN* contains the bibliographic information and article abstract exactly as they appear in *Psychological Abstracts*. Although the completeness of each entry reduces *PsycSCAN's* effectiveness as a timely current-awareness tool, the nonevaluative summaries can help you separate the truly relevant current journal literature from those with enticing, but occasionally misleading, titles.

2   Biographical Information

Sources Discussed

American Psychological Association. (1948–present). *Directory.* Washington, DC: Author. Triennial.

American Psychological Association. (1967–present). *Membership Register.* Washington, DC: Author. Annual (in years the *Directory* is not published).

Who's who in America. (1899/1900–present). Chicago: Marquis Who's Who. Biennial.

Who was who in America (7 vols.). (1943–present). Chicago: Marquis Who's Who. Irregular. Historical volume, which covers 1607 to 1896, plus 7 volumes, which cover the years to 1981.

History of psychology in autobiography (Vols. 1–4). (1930–1952). New York: Russell & Russell.

(Vol. 5). (1967). New York: Appleton-Century-Crofts.

(Vol. 6). (1974). Englewood Cliffs, NJ: Prentice-Hall.

(Vol. 7). (1980). San Francisco: W. H. Freeman.

Directories

Biographical directories can serve many purposes. They may provide current mailing addresses, lists of academic credentials, recent publications, and personal information, which may ease professional correspondence or be useful for the introduction of a speaker. You may find these directories useful for evaluating research by a particular author. Information on a psychologist's current research activities, credentials, and previous publications can be used to determine if an author has the background appropriate to the topic discussed in a journal article or book.

There are hundreds of biographical directories, each providing a different type of information and scope of coverage. Consequently, in this section we discuss a highly selective list of sources.

The primary purpose of the American Psychological Association's

Directory is to provide brief biographical data on APA members. Data are solicited by questionnaires sent to the membership; therefore, the amount of information provided for each individual varies. Entries are arranged by surname in the Main Alphabetic Section. Information about current address, academic credentials, major field of current research interest, present position, and so on is included in each entry.

In addition to providing information on individuals, the *Directory* contains a number of documents of interest to psychologists. Among these are statistics on APA membership, statements of principles and standards of professional practice, and the Association's bylaws. The *Directory* also contains a Geographical Index and a Divisional Membership Roster. Published in years when the *Directory* is not published, the *APA Membership Register* provides updated mailing addresses.

Almost every country is represented by a national biographical publication containing data on the country's more accomplished citizens, although the comprehensiveness and the frequency of these publications vary. One example is *Who's Who in America*, which contains vital statistics on prominent living Americans. *Who Was Who in America* offers similar brief biographical information on deceased Americans.

Other Sources

The *History of Psychology in Autobiography* presents a series of lengthy autobiographical essays by some of the most influential American psychologists. Each essay includes the life history of the person profiled as well as discussions of the person's important research and bibliographies of his or her selected publications. Because the essays reflect the psychologist's view of his or her research and of the discipline as a whole, they provide unique insights into each psychologist both as an individual and as a professional. Eminent psychologists included are, for example, S. S. Stevens, B. F. Skinner, G. W. Allport, R. S. Woodworth, and R. M. Yerkes. If you are a student of the history of psychology, this source may be of special interest to you.

T. S. Krawiec (1972, 1974, 1978) provides another similar set of autobiographical essays on 35 living psychologists. Each person included is distinguished in some area of psychology by his or her contributions through teaching, research, or writing. People included are, for example, A. Anastasi, R. B. Cattell, H. Helson, W. J. McKeachie, C. E. Osgood, P. Suppes, and R. I. Watson.

D. L. Sills (1979) includes biographies of 215 persons from the social sciences. Those selected for inclusion were major and influential forces in their respective fields. Essays were written by prominent academics in each field. Extensive bibliographies accompany each article.

3 Book Reviews

Sources Discussed

Contemporary psychology. (1956–present). Washington, DC: American Psychological Association. Monthly.

Book review index. (1965–present). Detroit: Gale Research. Bimonthly.

Chicorel index to mental health book reviews. (1974–present). New York: Chicorel. Annual.

Book reviews appearing in professional journals serve many purposes. Some faculty use reviews for selecting textbooks for college courses. Researchers regularly scan reviews for important new books in their fields of interest and to keep abreast of revised and updated editions of older publications. You may find reviews useful for evaluating a book's content and for placing it in the context of other available literature. Ideally, reviews are not limited to a description of a book's contents and a statement of recommendation or censure. Reviewers for scholarly journals are usually academics who are well acquainted with the literature in their respective fields. Therefore, they are able to evaluate a particular book in relation to other available literature.

The purpose of *Contemporary Psychology* is to provide evaluative reviews of current psychology materials, with a primary emphasis on books. Each issue contains lengthy reviews (between one and two pages) of approximately 55 titles and brief reviews of between 10 and 20 additional titles. Books are critiqued on their own merits and also evaluated in relation to existing psychological literature and thought. Each December issue contains an index, arranged by authors' and reviewers' names, to all reviews published during the year.

Reviews appearing in *Contemporary Psychology* and in more than 400 other scholarly journals and general-interest magazines are indexed in *Book Review Index.* Citations are arranged by book author or editor and by title. The number of journals and popular magazines indexed and the range of disciplines covered provide an excellent starting point for accessing book-review citations.

The *Chicorel Index to Mental Health Book Reviews* includes citations from only about 150 journals. It represents, however, a more specific focus than *Book Review Index:* It concentrates on reviews published in psychological, sociological, psychiatric, and medical journals. Reviews are indexed by author or editor, and each entry includes a brief description of the book's contents. Each volume also contains a brief subject index with authors or editors and book titles arranged under broad subject categories. Unfortunately, the usefulness of *Chicorel* is limited somewhat by its annual publication schedule.

References

Krawiec, T. S. (1972, 1974, 1978). *The psychologists* (3 vols.). New York: Oxford University Press.

Sills, D. L. (Ed.). (1979). *International encyclopedia of the social sciences: Biographical supplement.* New York: Free Press.

11 It's Not in the Library

Sources Discussed

Dissertation abstracts international. Part A: Humanities and social sciences. Part B: Sciences and engineering. (1938–present). Ann Arbor, MI: University Microfilms International. Monthly. *Part C: European abstracts.* (1976–present). Ann Arbor, MI: University Microfilms International. Quarterly.

Information industry market place: An international directory of information products and services. (1981–present). New York: Bowker. Annual.

Document retrieval: Sources and services (2nd ed.). (1982). San Francisco: The Information Store.

You have used indexes, abstracts, and other sources to compile a list of citations to relevant journal articles, books, and other materials. You have found some of these by checking the card catalog, the journal collection, government documents, and other resources. But your library may not own all of the research materials you need. This situation is not unusual. Because of the space needed for book, journal, and document storage and the high costs associated with purchase of books and subscription to journals, no library is able to own all of the materials needed for research by its community of faculty, students, and staff. This situation is true for small college libraries as well as for large, research-oriented university libraries.

After exhausting the resources of your library, then, where can you obtain additional materials? There are several options. Among these are interlibrary loan and document purchase.

Interlibrary Loan (ILL)

Libraries willing to assist one another in meeting the information needs of their users belong to one or more library networks that involve reciprocal agreements between libraries. Through these networks, a library may be able to obtain for one of its users a journal article, a book, or another publication that it does not own. Because of these networks, you may have access to a library located in another city or another state through a service known as interlibrary loan (ILL).

Interlibrary loan policies vary among libraries. Each library establishes its own guidelines based upon local funding, staffing, and other priorities. An interlibrary-loan librarian or a reference librarian will be able to inform you about local library policies. If you decide to use this service, you must keep in mind several things.

First, ILL takes time. Seldom can you obtain materials in less than two weeks. A rare journal or a book owned by only a few libraries (as may be the case for materials published in other countries or by small publishing houses) may involve a wait of a month or more. Thus you must begin your search early. Allow time to compile a list of references, to check your library's holdings, and to request materials through interlibrary loan. Once you receive these materials, you will need time to read and analyze them and to write your report.

Second, ILL procedures differ from library to library. Some libraries provide this service only to faculty members or to faculty and graduate students. Some networks do not provide services for student users. Therefore you must inquire about whether ILL is available to you.

Third, you must provide complete bibliographic information for the materials you wish to request. Such provision will not be a problem if you have consistently and accurately noted all the information you have found in an index or abstract entry. If you have not, you will need to retrace literature search steps to fill in the gaps in bibliographic information for each item requested.

Finally, some libraries charge for ILL service, especially for journal article requests. Libraries seldom lend an entire issue or a volume of a journal. Instead the article you need will be photocopied and mailed to your library. The cost for photocopying the article, as well as any service charge for locating the material, for postage, and so forth, may be passed on to you.

Typical ILL Procedures

After checking library policies, your next step is to decide what materials you really need to request. Given the time involved and possible monetary charges, you must identify essential sources and separate them from the nonessential (tangential, trivial, or redundant). Information contained in the abstracting and reviewing sources discussed in earlier chapters will help you evaluate the potential relevance of materials.

Once you have determined what materials you need, you must complete an ILL request form for each article, book, or other document. You can obtain this form from a reference or interlibrary-loan librarian. Your completed form will be the library's record of your request. Keep a record of materials that you have requested. Such a record will prevent duplicating requests, save you time and money, and let you know what material to expect.

To illustrate ILL procedures, we use the topic of "the reactions of children, as potential consumers, to television advertising." We identified citations in a manual search of *Psychological Abstracts* and the *Annual Review of Psychology*.

To illustrate a journal article request, we found entry 3457, an article by Scott Ward from the *Journal of Advertising Research*, in *PA*, Volume 49. The *PA* citation includes all information needed to complete an interlibrary-loan request. Figure 11–A presents a sample ILL request card completed for the Ward article. The information needed includes the name of the author (**1**), the article title (**2**), the journal title (**3**), the year of publication (**4**), the volume number (**5**), the issue and month (**6**), and the pages on which the article appears (**7**). In addition, the source in which the bibliographic information was located is provided (**8**). Some libraries will not process a request if information on the source is incomplete or omitted. Other information includes the date on which the request was placed (**9**), a date after which the material will no longer be usable (**10**), and the amount of money one is willing to pay for the duplication of the article (**11**). Additionally, there is space on the form for information identifying the person making the request (**12**). The form your library uses may be slightly different, but it will probably require the same kind of information.

Next we found an important book mentioned in an article by H. H. Kassarjian on consumer psychology, which appeared in the 1982 *Annual Review of Psychology*. Figure 11–B illustrates the ILL request for this book. As with the journal article, you must provide complete bibliographic information, including the names of the authors (**13**), the book title (**14**), the place of publication (**15**), the name of the publisher (**16**), and the date of publication (**17**). The source of the bibliographic information (**18**) is again requested, along with a date after which the book will no longer be usable (**19**). Note that in many respects the forms for book and journal requests are similar.

After submitting your request(s), inquire about notification procedures. Will the library telephone or write to you? Must you contact the library after a reasonable period of time to see if the materials

FIGURE 11–A

An interlibrary-loan journal-request form.

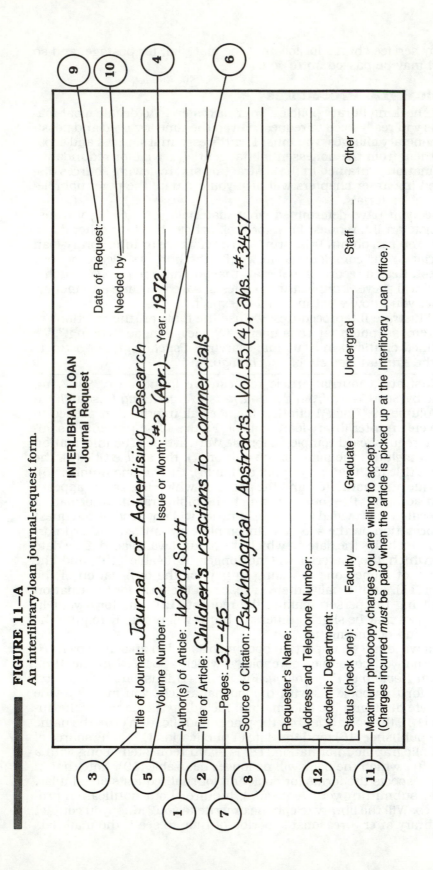

INTERLIBRARY LOAN
Journal Request

Date of Request: _____ ⑨

Needed by _____ ⑩

Title of Journal: *Journal of Advertising Research* ③

Volume Number: *12* ⑤ Issue or Month: *#2 (Apr.)* ① Year: *1972* ④

Author(s) of Article: *Ward, Scott* ②

Title of Article: *Children's reactions to commercials* ⑥

Pages: *37-45* ⑦

Source of Citation: *Psychological Abstracts, Vol.55 (4), abs. #3457* ⑧

Requester's Name: _____

Address and Telephone Number: _____ ⑫

Academic Department: _____

Status (check one): Faculty _____ Graduate _____ Undergrad _____ Staff _____ Other _____

Maximum photocopy charges you are willing to accept _____ ⑪
(Charges incurred *must* be paid when the article is picked up at the Interlibrary Loan Office.)

FIGURE 11–B
An interlibrary-loan book-request form.

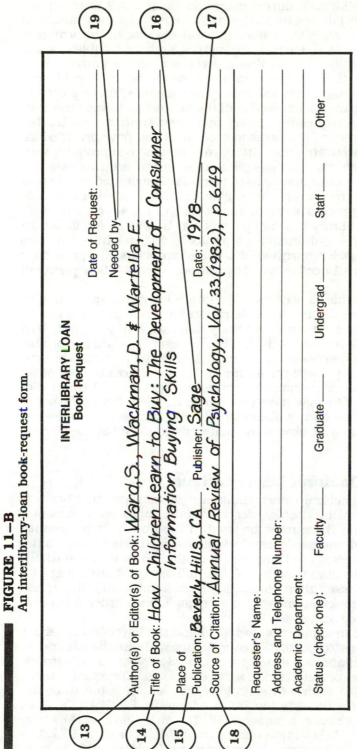

INTERLIBRARY LOAN
Book Request

Date of Request: _____

Needed by _____

Author(s) or Editor(s) of Book: *Ward,S., Wackman,D. & Wartella,E.*

Title of Book: *How Children Learn to Buy: The Development of Consumer Information Buying Skills*

Place of
Publication: *Beverly Hills, CA*   Publisher: *Sage*   Date: *1978*

Source of Citation: *Annual Review of Psychology, Vol. 33 (1982), p. 649*

Requester's Name: _____

Address and Telephone Number: _____

Academic Department: _____

Status (check one): Faculty _____ Graduate _____ Undergrad _____ Staff _____ Other _____

(13) (14) (15) (18) (19) (16) (17)

have been received? Also inquire about billing procedures and an estimated date of receipt of the materials.

Why does the ILL procedure consume so much time? Your request takes a tortuous journey involving many steps. Take the example of a journal-article request. A librarian will first locate information about the requested journal through a standard bibliographic source and identify a library that reports owning the journal. A request form will then be prepared and sent to the lending library. Staff in the lending library will locate the materials, make a copy of the article, prepare the bill, and mail the photocopy to your requesting library. The requesting library may then contact you. In this procedure, delays and problems may occur. If you have provided incomplete or inaccurate information, your request will probably wait while other requests with complete information are processed. A rare or obscure source may be hard to locate. The needed article may be missing from the library that is contacted. Any number of people involved in the process may make a mistake, or the source that indicated that XYZ library has your journal may be wrong. A holiday, an ill librarian, or a malfunctioning photocopying machine can also delay the process. Even without delays and problems, any procedure involving the mail needs time. The bottom line is—allow plenty of time!

If you are unable to wait for interlibrary loan and are willing to travel to another library, ask a librarian for assistance. He or she may be able to identify a nearby library that has what you need. This alternative must be used with caution, however. You will not be able to write or call other libraries and request that the materials be sent to you. Libraries provide photocopy and loan services only to other libraries, not to individuals. Some institutions restrict the use of their facilities: You may have to produce an identification card to gain access to the library. Although you will not be able to borrow materials, you may be able to use materials you need at the library.

Obtaining Doctoral Dissertations

Unlike books, doctoral dissertations are seldom lent by libraries. Universities granting doctoral degrees retain only a few copies of a dissertation, and these must be used in the library or in another archive. Instead, copies of most doctoral dissertations written in the United States are sent to University Microfilms International (UMI). Upon receipt of a dissertation, UMI microfilms it and announces its availability in *Dissertation Abstracts International (DAI)*. To request a copy of the dissertation, you must complete an order form and mail it with prepayment to UMI.

As illustrated in chapters 4 and 8, *PA* and the PsycINFO database contain citations to doctoral dissertations without the abstracts. Dissertation citations also appear in *Sociological Abstracts, Research/Resources in Education,* and so forth. Therefore, uncovering citations to several dissertations in a search is not unusual.

We identified a dissertation on our topic in *PA* (Vol. 55, April 1976), having the entry number 8552. The entry gave us the information that this dissertation was listed in *DAI,* February 1974, Volume 34, number 8-A, part 1, on pages 4489–4490. (*DAI* is pub-

FIGURE 11–C
Portions of an entry from *Dissertation Abstracts International*, 1974,
34(8-A, Pt. 1), 4489–4490.

(20) AN INVESTIGATION OF PREADOLESCENT CHILDREN'S
ATTITUDES TOWARD TELEVISION COMMERCIALS
(21) Clara Jean Potter FERGUSON, Ph.D.
North Texas State University, 1973 **(23)**

(22) The research efforts of commercial advertisers, television networks, and academicians have virtually ignored the effects of television commercials on the attitudes of preadolescent children. This
disregard is due primarily to the fact that this age group has not
been regarded as an important market segment. The child market,
however, has three important facets. First, preadolescent children
represent a substantial and significant consumer market for many

• • •

If television is to continue as an effective communication me-
dium for advertisers, and if television commercials are to stimulate
desired consumer behavior, appropriate action must be initiated by
advertising strategists. Negative attitudes already in existence must
be counteracted, and more positive attitudes toward television com- **(24)**
mercials must be cultivated.

Order No. 74–4030, 146 pages.

lished in three parts: Part A, *The Humanities and Social Sciences;*
Part B, *The Sciences and Engineering;* and Part C, *European Ab-
stracts.*) Because you can spend $20.00 or more on a single disserta-
tion, you should, for the sake of economy, consult the abstract in
DAI before deciding whether you wish to purchase the dissertation.
Many libraries do not purchase dissertations as a matter of policy.

Figure 11–C illustrates the entry from *DAI*. The title of the paper
(**20**), the name of the author (**21**), the institution granting the degree (**22**), and the year in which the degree was awarded (**23**) appear
at the beginning of the entry. Following this information is a lengthy
abstract describing the dissertation. At the end of the entry is the
order number (**24**), in case you decide to purchase the dissertation
microfilm from UMI. You may photocopy the order forms from recent
monthly issues of *DAI*.

Commercial Information Services

Another option, if you cannot or do not want to use ILL or to travel,
is employing an organization that provides copies of documents and
articles as a business. An advantage of this option is speed. Some
companies accept telephone requests, rush requests, and credit-
card payment for services. Some companies specialize in particular
subject areas or in rare documents. You can get the names and addresses of these organizations from either *Information Industry
Market Place* or *Document Retrieval: Sources and Services*. The
primary disadvantage of these sources, however, is cost: These serv-

ices are very expensive. To obtain a single journal article may cost you $10.00 or more, not including such special services as rush delivery. Therefore you must address the issues of how badly you need the information and how much it is worth to you.

If you have plenty of time and they are available to you, ILL services will meet almost all of your information needs not met by the local library.

Appendixes

A: Additional Specialized Sources
B: Brief Guide to Literature Searching

Appendix A: Additional Specialized Sources

This appendix lists and annotates a variety of sources not discussed within the book. This is a selected list: That is, we have attempted not to be inclusive but rather to illustrate the various types of sources available. Some sources are very specialized and, therefore, may not be available in your library. Other sources may be primarily of interest to teachers and researchers rather than to students. If you are interested in further information or in additional sources, consult McInnis (1982), listed below.

Psychology Bibliographies

McInnis, R. G. (1982). *Research guide for psychology.* Westport, CT: Greenwood Press.
  In more than 580 pages, this work lists and describes more than 1,200 bibliographic sources in psychology.
Watson, R. I., Sr. (Ed.). (1974). *Eminent contributors to psychology* (2 vols.). New York: Springer.
  Vol. 1: A bibliography of primary references.
  Vol. 2: A bibliography of secondary references.
  This reference tool is especially useful for the history of psychology.

Dictionaries and Encyclopedias

The following sources are useful in providing brief definitions and short articles. These books supplement handbooks mentioned in chapter 2.
American handbook of psychiatry (2nd ed., 7 vols.). (1974–1981). New York: Basic Books.
Eidelberg, L. (Ed.). (1968). *Encyclopedia of psychoanalysis.* New York: Free Press.
Koch, S. (Ed.). (1959–1963). *Psychology: A study of a science* (6 vols). New York: McGraw-Hill.
  Produced with the support of the American Psychological Association and the National Science Foundation, this series explores the foundations and the development of psychology and the relation of psychology to other sciences.
International encyclopedia of the social sciences (18 vols.). (1968). New York: Macmillan.
Wolman, B. B. (Ed.). (1978). *Dictionary of behavioral science.* New York: Van Nostrand Reinhold.
Wolman, B. B. (Ed.). (1977). *International encyclopedia of psychiatry, psychology, psychoanalysis and neurology* (12 vols.). New York: Van Nostrand Reinhold for Aesculapius Press.

Statistics Handbooks

The following handbooks contain numerous tables, many of which are not included in most statistics textbooks.
Beyer, W. H. (Compiler). (1968). *CRC handbook of tables for probability and statistics* (2nd ed.). Cleveland: Chemical Rubber Co.

Burrington, R. S., & May, D. C. (1970). *Handbook of probability and statistics with tables* (2nd ed.). New York: McGraw-Hill.

Directories

The following may be primarily of interest to researchers and faculty members. Use these sources with care because the information may change quickly.

American Psychological Association. (1981). *Guide to research support.* Washington, DC: Author.

Annual register of grant support. (1969–present). Chicago: Marquis. Annual.

Complete grants sourcebook for higher education. (1980). Washington, DC: American Council on Education.

Encyclopedia of associations. (1956–present). Detroit, MI: Gale. Annual.

Foundations directory (8th ed.). (1981). New York: The Foundation Center.

Research centers directory (7th ed.). (1982). Detroit, MI: Gale. Irregular.

Guides to Journals

Useful in deciding where to submit a manuscript, these guides include information about editorial policies of journals, acceptance rates, publication lag, and so forth. Information becomes outdated quickly in this area, so use these sources with care.

Author's guide to journals in psychology, psychiatry and social work. (1977). New York: Haworth.

Tompkins, M., & Shirley, N. (1976). *Serials in psychology and allied fields* (2nd ed.). Troy, NY: Whitston.

Indexes and Abstracts

Some of the following specialized services may be extremely useful. Because of their limited scope and the expense involved in subscribing to many possibly overlapping sources, however, these services may not be available through your library.

Animal behaviour abstracts. (1973–present). London: Informational Retrieval Ltd. Quarterly.

Child development abstracts and bibliography. (1927–present). Chicago: University of Chicago Press. Three times a year.

Criminal justice abstracts. (1969–present). Hackensack, NJ: National Council on Crime and Delinquency Information Center. Quarterly.

Criminal justice periodical index. (1975–present). Ann Arbor, MI: University Microfilms International. Annual.

Criminology and penology abstracts. (1961–present). Amsterdam, The Netherlands: Kugler. Bimonthly. (Formerly: *Abstracts on criminology and penology* and *Excerpta criminologica.)*

Excerpta medica: Section 32. Psychiatry. (1948–present). Amsterdam, The Netherlands: Excerpta Medica. Twenty times a year.

Excerpta medica: Section 40. Drug dependence. (1973–present). Amsterdam, The Netherlands: Excerpta Medica. Monthly.

Greenbaum, H. H., & Falcione, R. L. (1974–present). *Organizational communication: Abstracts, analysis, and overview.* Beverly Hills, CA: Sage. Annual.

Grinstein, A. (1956–1975). *Index of psychoanalytic writings* (14 vols.). New York: International Universities Press.

Index to current urban documents. (1972/1973–present). Westport, CT: Greenwood. Quarterly. This index covers publications issued by major American and Canadian cities and counties.

Index to periodical articles by and about Blacks. (1973–present). Boston: G. K. Hall. Annual. (Formerly: *Index to periodical articles by and about Negroes,* 1950–1972.)

LLBA: Language and language behavior abstracts. (1967–present). LaJolla, CA: Sociological Abstracts. Quarterly.

L'annee psychologique. (1894–present). Paris: Presses Universitaires de France. Semiannual.

Personnel literature. (1941–present). Washington, DC: U.S. Office of Personnel Management Library. Monthly. (Formerly issued by the U.S. Civil Service Commission Library.)

Psychopharmacology abstracts. (1961–present). Rockville, MD: National Institute of Mental Health, National Clearinghouse for Mental Health Information. Quarterly.

Women studies abstracts. (1972–present). Rush, NY: Rush Publishing. Quarterly.

General Bibliographies

You can use the following sources to check on the current availability of books.

Books in print. (1948–present). New York: Bowker. Annual.

Forthcoming books. (1966–present). New York: Bowker. Bimonthly.

Publisher's trade list annual. (1872–present). New York: Bowker. Annual.

Subject guide to books in print. (1957–present). New York: Bowker. Annual.

Subject guide to forthcoming books. (1967–present). New York: Bowker. Bimonthly.

Supplement to books in print. (1972/1973–present). New York: Bowker. Annual.

National Bibliographies

You will find that the primary function the following sources serve is verification of the accuracy of bibliographic information about a particular source. They attempt to be inclusive, covering all materials published and copyrighted in the United States or held by American libraries.

National union catalog, pre-1956 imprints (681 vols.). (1967–1980). London: Mansell. *Supplement* (69 vols.). (1980–1981).

National union catalog: A cumulative author list representing Library of Congress printed cards and titles reported by other American libraries. (1956–present). Washington, DC: Library of

Congress. Monthly, cumulated annually and quinquenially. [1953–1957 (26 vols.); 1956–1962 (50 vols.); 1963–1967 (59 vols.); 1968–1972 (104 vols.); 1973–1977 (135 vols.)] (Publisher varies)

Library of Congress. (1975–present). *Subject catalog.* Washington, DC: Author. Quarterly.

Library of Congress Catalog. Books: Subjects; A cumulative list of works represented by Library of Congress printed cards. [1950–1954 (20 vols.); 1955–1959 (22 vols.); 1960–1964 (25 vols.); 1965–1969 (42 vols.); 1970–1974 (100 vols.)] (Publisher varies)

Union list of serials in libraries of the United States and Canada (3rd ed.) (5 vols.). (1965). New York: H. W. Wilson.

New serial titles: A union list of serials commencing publication after December 31, 1949. (1953–present). Washington, DC: Library of Congress. Monthly.

1950–1970 Cumulative (4 vols.). (1973).

1971–1975 Cumulation (2 vols.). (1976).

1976–1980 Cumulation (2 vols.). (1981).

New serial titles. Classed subject arrangement. (1955–present). Washington, DC: Library of Congress. Monthly.

Appendix B: Brief Guide to Literature Searching

The step-by-step guidelines provided below will help you organize and conduct a literature search. Complete each section in sequential order. Record actual sources located in the search on individual index cards as suggested in chapter 1. In parentheses are the chapters in which particular steps in the process and bibliographic resources are discussed.

Stage 1. Defining and Limiting the Topic (chapter 2)

- State the general topic.
- Briefly define the topic.
- Provide an initial source or reference.
- Find a review source for general background:
    Textbook
    Annual review
    Handbook
- Limit the topic by one or more of the following:
    Sub-area
    Theory
    Species
    Research methodology
    Time period
    Other
- State the narrowed topic statement or research question.
- Are there further possibilities for limitation? What are these?
- Ask self-analyzing questions:
    What do you find most interesting about this topic?
    Why are you interested in this area?
- State the narrowed topic.
- List original primary sources (journal articles, authors, etc.).
- List subject-search terms.

Stage 2. Finding Books (for a general overview and possible important new contributions to the topic area; chapter 3)

- List important authors and titles to consult.
- List subject headings for card catalog.

Stage 3. Finding Research in Journal Articles with a Subject Search (chapters 4 & 5)

- List the sources to be consulted (depending on area).
    Psychological Abstracts
    ERIC *CIJE* & *RIE* or *EI*
    BPI
    Sociological Abstracts
    Index Medicus
    Biological Abstracts
    Others (see appendix)

- Consult a thesaurus (if available): List acceptable subject headings for the topic. (Modify the list, as needed, while conducting the search.)
- List bibliographic sources consulted.

Stage 4. Searching by Author/Citation in Addition to or Instead of by Subject (chapter 6)

- Answer the following questions. If you answer "yes" to each, proceed using *SSCI*. If you answer "no" to the questions, a citation search will not be helpful.
  Do you have access to *SSCI*?
  Do you have an important initial reference critical to early development of the field? If "yes," what is the reference?

Stage 5. Locating Relevant Government Documents (chapter 7)

- Ask yourself whether this is an area in which governmental agencies have an interest. If "yes," then
  Check the *Monthly Catalog*.
  Check the *Index to U.S. Government Periodicals*.

Stage 6. Considering a Computer Search (chapter 8)

- Before requesting a search, consider the following questions:
  Is this service available to you?
  Is there a charge involved? If so, how much?
  Is the search worth doing?
  Do you have enough time to wait for the results?
- If you decide to proceed, do the following:
  Find out who to contact.
  Decide which available database should be searched.
  Prepare a search strategy, including all of the information gathered in Stages 1 and 3 above.

Stage 7. Locating Materials Not in the Library (chapter 10)

- Before requesting interlibrary loan services, ascertain the following:
  Is interlibrary loan service available to you?
  Which unavailable materials do you really need?
  Is there a charge for the service? If so, how much?
  How long will you have to wait for the materials?
- If able to proceed based on the answers to questions, then do the following:
  Record complete and accurate bibliographic information on each source you request.
  Keep a record of each source requested.
  Ask if, when, and how you will be notified about receipt of the materials.

Index

Italic page numbers indicate figures (e.g., *77*). ***Italic bold page numbers*** indicate tables (e.g., ***77***).